WHY I RUN

WHY I RUN

35 PROGRESSIVE CANDIDATES

★ ★ ★ WHO ARE ★ ★ ★

CHANGING POLITICS

EDITED BY
KATE CHILDS GRAHAM

ABRAMS IMAGE, NEW YORK

Contents

Foreword

TAMMY DUCKWORTH

U.S. Senate // Illinois // Elected in 2016

ON NOVEMBER 4, 2008, Barack Obama became the first African American to win the United States presidency. Late that evening, he stood at a podium in Chicago's Grant Park and said to the 200,000 Americans gathered there that his victory belonged to all of us.

More than eight years later, after serving two terms as our president, he returned to Chicago to give his farewell address. The atmosphere had a different charge. Yes, there was a lot to celebrate—big achievements like the Affordable Care Act, marriage equality, Deferred Action for Childhood Arrivals (DACA), Wall Street reform, and the end of the war in Iraq. Not to mention that our country was finally recovering from the Great Recession.

But that night, the celebration was mixed with apprehension. There was a new president just days from being sworn in. A man who had risen to power while attacking women, people of color, immigrants, people with disabilities, and prisoners of war—all while seeming to embrace enemies foreign (Russia) and domestic (hate groups). It felt as if all the progress we'd made was on the line.

Across the country, people were scared and angry and restless. President Obama understood that. He probably felt some of that himself, too. So, that night, he challenged the American people. He called on us to do more, saying that our democracy needed us—all of us.

"If you're disappointed by your elected officials, grab a clipboard, get some signatures, and run for office yourself," President Obama said. "Show up. Dive in. Persevere. Sometimes you'll win. Sometimes you'll lose."

Within a year of that speech, tens of thousands of people had signed up to run for office. Not just career politicians with deep campaign coffers but people who were brand-new to politics, people who didn't have a seat at the table before. And by the first anniversary of President Donald Trump's inauguration, these progressive candidates had flipped dozens of legislative seats from red to blue.

Running for office is tough, and winning can be even tougher—especially if you don't fit the expected mold. This reality can be particularly discouraging when you consider that we'd just witnessed an incredibly qualified candidate—the inimitable, inspiring Hillary Clinton—lose the presidential election. It was a crushing blow, but these progressive candidates forged ahead, undaunted. All with their own stories, their own missions driving them forward.

My story began with my military service.

November 12, 2004, is my "Alive Day." It was the day I almost died but didn't—and it was a good day for me. I was flying high over Iraq in my Black Hawk with the best crew out there when, without warning, a rocket-propelled grenade tore through the cockpit of my helicopter.

It was a lucky shot for the enemy. One of my legs was vaporized, and the other amputated by my helicopter's instrument panel. The explosion blew off the entire back of my right arm. I was, quite literally, in pieces. My pilot-in-command managed to land our aircraft, and the crew started pulling out the wounded.

They thought I was dead at first, but when they tried to give medical attention to one of my crew members, Chris, he refused help and told them to assist me instead. He saw that I was still bleeding and realized that maybe my heart was still beating.

OUR DEMOCRACY TAKES ALL OF US AND THAT'S **WHY WE RUN**

He did what every service member in combat is willing to do, even if they hope they never have to: He refused treatment for himself to save someone else.

My buddies wouldn't give up on me. They refused to leave me behind. They picked me up, covered in blood and tissue, and tried to keep my body intact.

It was a good day for me because good men saved me and I lived. I survived to serve my nation again.

The days, weeks, and months that followed were some of the hardest of my life. But in those challenging moments, my life's mission couldn't have been clearer. I knew from that moment on that I would spend every single day of the rest of my life trying to honor the courage and sacrifice of those who had saved me that day. So, with the help of my family, friends, and fellow service members at Walter Reed, I began my recovery.

It was anything but easy. Tasks like picking up a pencil or even just sitting up without passing out were no longer simple. At first, it was unclear how I would lead a regular life, let alone continue serving my nation. But I decided not to give up. It wasn't a choice, really, because giving up would have been a betrayal of the effort my buddies had put into saving me, and I knew I couldn't betray them.

So, I got back up, I dusted myself off, and I got back into the arena. I may have been broken, but I could still be an Army officer. I could still take care of my troops. Maybe I was done serving in combat, but I could see that the next step in my life's path still meant serving my fellow veterans.

After I got out of Walter Reed, I went to work at the Department of Veterans Affairs, I ran for Congress, and then I won my seat in the Senate. I was sworn into the Senate just days before President Trump took his oath of office.

I ran for Congress because I felt I had a debt to repay to those men who'd saved my life. And whenever things get tough, I just think of them, and I keep going.

When running for office, I've found that the "why" often explains the "how." That's certainly true of the stories you'll read here.

In these pages, you'll hear from a refugee who is now a mayor in rural America, a black woman who confronted voters who were wearing

Confederate flags on the campaign trail, and a mom who wants her transgender daughter to be able to use the girls' bathroom at school. You'll learn from incredible people and unlikely leaders who have stepped up to serve their communities.

They all grabbed a clipboard. They all ran for office. They showed up. They dove in. They persevered. Some won. And some lost.

The people in this book—and so many others—are changing the face of politics in our country. I've often said that if we want to make our democracy more representative, our leaders need to look more like the people we represent. But the fact is that, traditionally, certain people have been shut out of politics in our country. Studies have shown that women, for instance, are less likely than men to think about running for office. They are less likely to be encouraged to run, too. I'm thankful that that's starting to change.

I was at the Women's March the day after the inauguration. I wore my "Don't F--- With Me" jacket. I had my daughter with me. She was two at the time, and it was her first protest. I asked the crowd not to let the energy fade after that day. I asked them to build on that energy. To act. To run for office. To be the change we want to see. And I'm so proud that so many have done just that.

President Obama was right. Our democracy takes all of us. And that's why we run.

Introduction

KATE
CHILDS GRAHAM

EVERYONE HAS A STORY about the 2016 election.

My story is about the 2017 elections.

I went to sleep knowing that Ralph Northam had won the governor's race in Virginia and that Phil Murphy had won in New Jersey. When I woke up the next morning, I looked at my phone and learned that that was just the beginning. In Virginia, New Jersey, Washington, Montana, Kansas—in states across the country—progressive Americans who had stepped up to run for office, many of them for the first time, won.

Ravi Bhalla. Danica Roem. Kathy Tran. Melvin Carter. Wilmot Collins. Justin Fairfax. Jenny Durkan. Sheila Oliver. Michelle De La Isla. Andrea Jenkins. The list scrolled down my screen.

I read their stories. I read their stories again.

They were activists and teachers, doctors and parents, students and veterans. They were from cities and towns, red and blue. They'd run for every office imaginable. They'd run on big, bold platforms. Some ran against longtime, right-wing incumbents. Many refused to take corporate PAC money. And they won.

They were women, people of color, and queer people. They ran for office right after America failed to put the first woman president, the most qualified candidate we've seen in generations, in the White House. That takes guts.

As a speechwriter, I've read a lot of politicians' stories. But these were different. No poll-tested platitudes. (I doubt some of them could even afford to put a poll in the field.) No timeworn truisms. The candidates weren't always refined, but they were clear: We love our communities. We believe in progress. We want to serve. And we'll do whatever it takes.

They woke me up from what felt like a year of dreaming—or, more accurately, a waking nightmare. Like everyone else, I was doing what I could, but I wasn't pushing myself. Not the way they were.

I asked myself what more I could do. This book is my answer.

We were getting most of their stories in snippets. Scrolling through our Twitter feeds. Listening to NPR while driving. Watching MSNBC while making dinner. After a news cycle or two, the stories faded away. But on November 7, 2017, these brave people didn't just make national news. They made history. So on November 8, I decided that that history deserved to be written down by the people who'd made it and continue to make it.

Why had they run? What platform had they run on? Whom had they run for? How had they won? And if they hadn't won, what had they learned?

As I collected these essays, I realized that the stories here give us more than a record of what happened. They help guide us through a time of profound political change. In the days following the 2017 elections, there were a lot of one-note headlines about the candidates who'd won. "Elections Bring Wins for Minority, LGBT Candidates," said CNN. "A Year After Trump, Women and Minorities Give Groundbreaking Wins to Democrats," declared the *New York Times*.

We read the same things after the 2018 elections. About Debra Haaland and Sharice Davids, the first Native American women elected to Congress. And Ilhan Omar and Rashida Tlaib, the first Muslim women elected to Congress. And Alexandria Ocasio-Cortez, the youngest congresswoman in history. About the record-breaking number of women and LGBTQ people who ran. And the glass-ceiling-breaking number who won.

WHY NOT RUN?

It was, and is, exciting. And yet, the diverse identities of progressive candidates represent only part of the story. The bigger story is about how these progressive candidates are changing politics by renewing our faith in it. By bringing those who have been disenfranchised back into the fold— and to the polls. By teaching us to think big, moon-shot big. By inspiring a new generation of leaders to serve.

By some counts, there are more than half a million elected officials in the United States. Tens of thousands of progressive candidates have stepped up to run, and there's room for hundreds of thousands more.

So if you find yourself asking what more you can do, let me ask you this—

Why not run?

STACEY ABRAMS

Governor // Georgia // Candidate in 2018

MY PARENTS RAISED MY FIVE siblings and me with three tenets: go to school, go to church, and take care of one another.

Service was a way of life for us. My mother and father instilled in us the idea that no matter how little we had, someone else had less—and it was our job to help care for those people. I did not even realize, as a child, that Saturday was a day off for most children. We spent ours in soup kitchens and juvenile justice centers. When we had a neighbor in need, we would lend a hand. But I could never understand why it was not someone else's job to help and to make bigger changes in people's lives.

Back then, just as is true too often now, our elected leaders were not always responsive to the needs of the people they were meant to serve. They did not always invest in making sure that every family has opportunity, no matter who they are or where they live. And so it fell to others, like my parents, to fill the gap and support those who needed it.

My family's dedication to helping people led me to think about the ways that our government could better help people. It opened my eyes to the impact public servants can and should make—and to how our leaders often failed to fulfill their promises. I saw the power that elected leaders could wield. I saw the power that a governor could wield.

* * *

The first time I visited the governor's mansion in Georgia, they almost didn't let me in.

I was seventeen years old and valedictorian of the Avondale High School Class of 1991. Like every valedictorian in the state, I was invited to meet the governor. I woke up on the day of the event and put on my best dress. I put on heels, as well, at my mother's request—even though I hated wearing them. And I got on the bus with my mom and my dad. Our car had broken down when we moved to Georgia, so, like a lot of other families, we used public transportation to get around.

We got off the bus on West Paces Ferry Road, where the governor's mansion is, and started walking up this long driveway as we watched the other valedictorians and their families drive up. Before we got to the house, we approached a big pair of gates and a security guard.

My dad introduced me as one of the valedictorians, but the guard looked at my family and said, "No. This is a private event. You're not allowed. You don't belong."

He did not want to let us in. But that guard had never met Robert or Carolyn Abrams. After a vigorous discussion, he checked his list and let us enter through the gates.

I don't remember meeting the governor or even my fellow valedictorians. But what I do remember was the feeling of being told that I could not have something I had earned. The feeling that, because of where I came from, I would be left out, unable to walk through those gates.

I decided to run for governor because I want to swing those gates wide open for every Georgian.

* * *

After my visit to the governor's mansion, I attended Spelman College, followed by the University of Texas Lyndon B. Johnson School of Public Policy and Yale Law School.

At every step, I found ways to step up and serve.

During high school, for instance, I was hired as a typist for a congressional campaign. One day, I took it upon myself to tweak one speech as I typed it up. The campaign manager liked what I wrote and promoted me to speechwriter.

During college, I got involved with the activism that was happening on campus, helping organize protests around the police treatment of Rodney King. When local police teargassed my campus, I decided to take action. I told the mayor of Atlanta at the time, Maynard Jackson, that he was not listening to the voices of young people. Six months later, he offered me a job in the city's department of youth services, where I focused on gang prevention and youth civic engagement efforts.

In law school, I offered to help the friend of a friend set up his non-profit helping formerly incarcerated individuals—many who were HIV positive—get jobs converting hotels into apartments. I had taken exactly one tax law class, but my friend promised that was more than he knew. Every week, I would trek from New Haven to New York to fill out his paperwork. I found that tax law allowed me to use both the left and right sides of my brain, and so it became my specialty.

After law school, I worked at a white-shoe law firm. I exceeded my pro bono hours every month. Still, I kept thinking about my parents, about that drive to serve. So I left the private sector to become deputy city attorney of Atlanta. At age twenty-nine, I was the youngest person ever to hold that role.

But what I really wanted to do, more than anything, was to end poverty in Georgia. I came to realize that a job with the City of Atlanta was just not going to foster that change.

When State Representative JoAnn McClinton announced that she would not run for reelection in 2006, I decided to run for her seat. I faced two opponents, but I reached out to as many voters as I could. And because people respond when you work hard, listen to their concerns, and offer solutions to their challenges, I earned their votes, and I won.

Just four years later, I was elected to lead the Democratic caucus in the statehouse. I was the first woman to lead either party in the Georgia General Assembly and the first African American to lead the state House of Representatives.

I believe that to get ahead in politics, you can't just talk. You need to listen to everyone, and you need to have a record that you can be proud of.

I worked to include voices that were too often left out, and I was able to accomplish more than many legislators serving in the minority. The local paper even called me "strangely relevant." But, really, my work wasn't so strange. It was rooted in what I'd learned from my mom and dad.

My parents were activists in the civil rights movement. Like so many, they fought tirelessly to secure the right to vote. My father even registered voters before he was old enough to vote himself, because he knew being able to exercise your voice at the ballot box was vital. That is why, when I found out that more than 800,000 people of color in Georgia were not registered to vote, I knew I had to do something. I founded an organization called the New Georgia Project, which has submitted voter registration forms from more than 200,000 people of color in Georgia and successfully fought voter suppression.

And I helped build Democratic power in the state. As House minority leader, I recruited, trained, and worked to elect Democrats to the statehouse. We flipped six seats drawn for Republicans—and I started to understand what it takes to win elections in my state.

After that, I launched my campaign for governor. Now, some said that was foolhardy. They said that Georgia hadn't been "blue" since 1992. That our last Democratic governor left office in 2003. And that no black woman has ever been governor of any state in the United States.

But I was ready to imagine more for our state. And here's what I learned along the way: Georgians don't have to soften our commitment to equality and opportunity to win. We just have to be architects of real, bold solutions. We just have to show that our elected leaders can, at their best, bring people together to help one another.

I really believe that, because that's how I was raised.

Before we moved to Georgia, we lived in Gulfport, Mississippi. My mom was a college librarian. My dad was a shipyard worker. We were working class, working poor. But even when we struggled, we always tried to support our neighbors.

My dad would often take a second shift. We had only one car, so my mom would pile all the kids into it and take us to pick him up. He would walk to meet us partway, and my siblings and I would look out the windows to see if we could find him.

One cold night when we picked him up, we all noticed he didn't have his coat. My dad told us that he had met a man without a coat and so he gave him his. He told us, "That man was alone then and I knew that he'd be alone when I left, but I knew you were coming for me."

Our parents taught us to take care of one another. They taught us to serve. That's why I ran.

AMY MCGRATH

U.S. House of Representatives //
Kentucky's 6th Congressional District // Candidate in 2018

★

WHEN I WAS A YOUNG GIRL growing up in Kentucky, I dreamed of being a fighter pilot. But women couldn't do that then. A federal law prohibited us from serving in combat roles.

I wrote a letter to my congressman, asking him to change the law. He wrote back and explained that Congress thought women should not be allowed to serve in these roles. I just couldn't accept that answer. So I wrote to every member of the armed services committees in the U.S. House of Representatives and Senate. Some, like Senator Mitch McConnell, never responded. A few others did. It was a lesson in perseverance, and also in government.

Representative Patricia Schroeder of Colorado wrote, "The object of a war is to win. We should, therefore, field the best-qualified military possible . . . I think that it is time for military service to be based on qualifications, not gender."

Thanks to leaders like her, by the time I was eighteen years old the law had changed, and the doors were open for me to do what I wanted to do in the military. Still, I will never forget that feeling of being shut out, of being discriminated against because of my gender, of not being allowed the opportunity to follow my dream.

I attended the United States Naval Academy at a time when many did not think women should have a place in such an institution. Four long, tough years later, I was commissioned as an officer in the United States Marine Corps, and my dream to serve as an F/A-18 fighter pilot came true.

The academy and the Marine Corps did more than teach me to fly; they instilled values, a desire to serve my country, and a code of conduct I carry with me—honor, courage, and commitment. I have lived by that code for more than twenty-four years.

I completed flight school in 1999 and reported to Marine Corps Air Station Miramar in San Diego, California. Two years after that, on the morning of September 11, 2001, I spent four hours strapped into an F/A-18 loaded with air-to-air missiles, awaiting orders to shoot down any commercial airliner believed to be headed for a terrorist attack in Los Angeles or San Diego. I was deployed to Afghanistan and Iraq more than once. All told, I flew about two thousand flight hours and eighty-nine combat missions.

Throughout my military service, I learned to be a servant-leader. That means someone who puts others before self, prioritizing your group's needs before your own. It means doing the hard things before you ask anyone else to do them, living every day with the principles of character, trustworthiness, and integrity that you want to see in others. It means stepping up and taking responsibility.

Somewhere in my career—maybe it was as a midshipman, maybe it was later on as an officer in the Marine Corps—I realized how lucky I was to have been surrounded by amazing leaders. They taught me real leadership by example, by how they lived their lives, by how they led their Marines. I learned to lead from them. It's as simple as that.

When I realized I had been given a gift in having seen so many different types of good leaders (and even some bad), I knew I had to use the skills I had been taught. I knew I had to use the moral compass my parents gave me as a child. And I wanted to follow these words, from the Gospel of Luke, that became my motto: "To whom much has been given, much is expected."

Before I decided to run for Congress, I was assigned to teach the principles of our Constitution and the United States government to young midshipmen at the Naval Academy. These students were the future leaders of our Navy and Marine Corps and the future leaders of our country.

As the elections of 2016 unfolded, it was more and more difficult to explain what was happening—especially to these young Americans who were stepping up to serve on the front lines of our nation's wars, risking their lives.

I found myself feeling disappointed in my country in a way I had never experienced before—the "fake news," the personal attacks, the lack of truth and decency, the influence of foreign powers on our democracy, and the divisiveness. This was not the character of the country for which I had fought as a Marine.

The moment when I said, "That's it, I'm running," was the day after the 2016 elections. I woke up that morning feeling as if someone had sucker punched me. I had a hole in my heart, in a place where I used to be so proud. There was a sickness I found difficult to describe.

I'd served our country my entire adult life. I'd lost friends who'd served. I felt that I couldn't just sit back and accept the new reality—especially when I saw the shrinking confidence my students had in our elected leaders.

My students now assumed that our elected leaders were simply out for themselves or for their party. Personal honor no longer appeared to mean much in political discourse. Politicians were just not doing the right thing anymore.

The new commander-in-chief stood for essentially the opposite of almost everything I had stood for my entire life. For a woman in the military, the idea of having someone so degrading to women, so degrading to the military, to public servants, to the idea of selfless service, to honesty in such high office—well, my response was something like, "Oh, hell no." In that moment, I knew that there would be a day when I would run for office.

But the "when" came a little later. It came when the Republicans started trying to push through their "repeal and replace" of the Affordable Care Act in the spring of 2017. I knew this was politically motivated, because they didn't have a plan to replace it. They just wanted a repeal, and they were lying to people about what their "replace" plan would do.

Kentucky, my home, was the largest beneficiary of the Medicaid-expansion portion of the Affordable Care Act. To me, the Republican leaders from Kentucky were absolutely hurting their own. That's when I decided to run.

My husband and I were reaching the age in the military when we could retire. We knew we wanted to move back to Kentucky, where I was from, to be closer to family. The time was right. The time was now.

I always felt that it was my duty to serve in some capacity. The first part of my adult life was defined by service to my country in the military and service to my fellow Marines. The second part of my adult life could be another form of service, to my fellow Kentuckians, but also a continued service to my country—this time in politics.

We need more real leaders in politics. Not just career politicians but people who have served in lots of different ways. For me, running for office was absolutely the right thing to do and the right way to continue my service.

This is my next mission.

WE NEED MORE
★ REAL ★
LEADERS
➤ IN ◄
POLITICS

KWAME RAOUL

Attorney General // Illinois // Elected in 2018

★

WHEN I FIRST WALKED INTO the Illinois capitol as a state senator, I was there to replace a man named Barack Obama. It was November 2004, and he'd been elected to the U.S. Senate. Inevitably someone would tell me that I had big shoes to fill, and I took to responding in a particular way.

"I respect Barack too much to have him walking around Washington, D.C., barefoot," I'd say, "so I'll let him keep his shoes, and I'll keep wearing the shoes that brought me to the table in the first place."

I'm not the next Barack Obama. I'm the first Kwame Raoul.

My parents immigrated from Haiti, which you may remember as one of the countries President Trump called a "shithole." The denigration of Haitian Americans didn't start with Trump; he was just more honest about it than most.

When my father finished his medical training in pathology at the top of his class and applied to work in hospitals, they didn't see his education or talent; all they saw was the color of his skin. So he became a community physician on the South Side of Chicago, serving the area's diverse neighborhoods for the next thirty years. He never turned away a patient who was unable to pay. He would sometimes come home with a block of cheese or fruitcake; sometimes a patient would offer to fix our plumbing.

He would accept these gifts and care for people he knew could never repay him, because he understood health care to be a human right, not a privilege for those who could afford it.

I was appointed to the state senate exactly one year after my father's death. He never ran for office, and I never followed him into medicine, but I sought to emulate his public service and work ethic.

* * *

I was a college student when Chicago elected its first African American mayor, Harold Washington, and I was impressed with his intellect, communication skills, and the way he adapted his approach to the city's various communities to build a coalition for progressive advocacy. When the mayor passed away, I keenly felt that so much had been gained and then so quickly lost. Inspired by his example, I went to law school to become an advocate for the voiceless and pledged to myself that I would be open to service through elected office. In 1995, one year after obtaining my law degree, I ran for Chicago City Council against someone who is one of my closest friends, mentors, and political allies today: Toni Preckwinkle, now president of the Cook County Board of Commissioners. At the time, she represented my ward on the city council.

I lost.

Naively, I equated being equipped academically with being equipped politically. But some activists took notice of my ability to engage young professionals in politics, and they persuaded me to run for the state senate. At the time, my supermajority African American district was represented by a white senator, and I thought I could more effectively speak for my community. Again, I was naive and underestimated what it took to put together a campaign. I mastered the issues and picked up major endorsements and thought that would work.

I lost again.

In 1999, I ran once more against Alderwoman Preckwinkle.

And once again, I was trounced. The third time was not the charm.

In the soul-searching that followed, I returned to the root of my aspirations: my desire to serve. I wrote to Toni Preckwinkle that I'd made a mistake by running against her, because, honestly, there weren't many differences between us. Then I volunteered to help out in the Fourth Ward. I started running a legal clinic out of Toni's office, then worked with Fifth Ward Alderwoman Leslie Hairston to expand its reach. I was approached about running for a judgeship, but this time I took a pass and chose to spend more time with my father, who was dying from metastasized prostate cancer.

A year later, sadder and wiser, when Obama vacated his state senate seat and I was asked to put in my name, I was ready. I proved I was serious, raising money and reaching out to the elected members of the committee who would vote on the appointment.

When I prevailed, many Springfield insiders were surprised; they thought a different candidate, preferred by the state senate president and other insiders, was a shoo-in. Instead, they got me.

At first, lobbyists would come to my office assuming I'd support a bill because my predecessor had. Instead, I broke the news to them that they were dealing with a different person. Our politics were similar but not identical. People who wanted things in Springfield found out they would need to make their case to me, not just mention Obama's name. I would tell them, "Barack is in D.C. now and took his gray matter with him, so you're relegated to appealing to the brain with which my parents blessed me."

When I began serving in the senate, I thought the merits of my positions were all I needed to persuade others. I had to learn to appreciate incremental change and people who found common cause with me but for different reasons. But gradual changes accumulate. I'm amazed at how perspectives have evolved on so many seemingly intractable issues.

One way to make a difference as a public servant is being willing to negotiate "middle of the highway issues"—the kind that make you feel like you're standing in the middle of a highway, because people are coming at you from both directions. Another way is to work on topics that aren't politically sexy.

Soon after I started serving in the state senate, I had an interesting conversation with the then president Emil Jones in the bathroom, of all places. He told me that most minority legislators seek out appointments to committees dealing with social issues—public health, human services, or education, for example. But it's important to look beyond obvious avenues of assistance, he said, because too often they're Band-Aids on a larger problem. If you want to make an impact, he said, follow the money. Look at economic opportunity and the hard realities that create and destroy it.

I started holding hearings on the participation of minority-owned and women-owned financial services firms in the investment of state assets. It is an injustice to presume that individuals of all races are good enough to pay into state pension funds but not to manage that money. Illinois now leads nationally in giving disadvantaged businesses a fair chance to compete for a share in the allocation of public pension fund assets to manage. Our efforts don't garner much publicity, but they've created tangible opportunities for Illinoisans facing barriers to economic participation.

* * *

Being a son has had a profound effect on my approach to policy making, and so has being a father. I raised my two children in the same neighborhood where I grew up. I've heard gunfire on our block and feared for their safety, and one afternoon I had to ask another family to take my son to their house after basketball practice because I hadn't yet figured out how to tell him that a thirteen-year-old boy had been shot just across the street from our home.

Both my kids sustained multiple concussions in high school sports. While I was working on legislation addressing accommodations for students with concussions, I was experiencing the effects of concussion on my own children and struggling to communicate their needs to educators who didn't fully comprehend the nature of their injuries.

Public policy became personal again when I was diagnosed with prostate cancer—the same disease that took my father and both grandfathers from me. Early detection and excellent medical care saved my life. I'd always championed health-care access, by cosponsoring the legislation authorizing Illinois to expand Medicaid under the Affordable Care Act, for example. My diagnosis caused me to redouble my commitment to ensuring that everyone has the fighting chance I had.

At the heart of representative democracy are citizen legislatures composed not of specially trained experts but of ordinary women and men who bring their life experiences to bear on their policy making.

I've been known to express myself emotionally in the public square; more than once I've shed tears. My sensitivity to immigration policy is influenced by my parents' journey, my fight for affordable health care has taken shape through my father's legacy and my own health challenges, and my commitment to a woman's right to choose and equal rights for women is strengthened by the dreams I have for my daughter.

I put my name on a ballot again—this time for Illinois attorney general—after fourteen years in the state senate because the sum total of my personal and professional experiences gave me the capacity and motivation to serve in a position that is more indispensable now than perhaps at any other time in our country's history.

Public servants are human beings, and we should never pretend we aren't. When voters complain that they are tired of politicians, often what they mean is that they're tired of candidates and officials who try to fit themselves into a standard mold. If I were to advise someone considering running for public office, I would offer this: Know yourself before you recommend yourself to others in service. Your community doesn't need another Lincoln, King, or Obama. It needs you.

HELEN GYM

City Council // Philadelphia, Pennsylvania // Elected in 2015

ONE OF THE EARLIEST LESSONS I learned in my life was that you have to build the world you want, not the one before you.

I learned that from my Korean immigrant parents, who had left behind almost everything to come to the United States—family, culture, language. Like so many immigrants, my parents created their own sense of belonging by building a community for me and my sister and themselves, whether through Sunday church services or social and cultural gatherings.

I learned that while teaching in desperately underfunded and overcrowded public schools, organizing and working with teachers and educators, student groups and advocates, to keep pushing for the schools our children both need and deserve.

And I learned that most of all from a group of radical Asian American activists who shaped the political and organizing spirit that has guided me throughout my life.

As a young adult, I walked into a tiny storefront in Philadelphia's Chinatown called Asian Americans United (AAU). A friend of mine told me that I had to get to know the women there who could "change the world."

And just like my parents before me, I knew I had found my community.

The board of AAU included men and women who had been part of the civil rights struggle, who had mobilized against apartheid and nuclear power, who had fought for LGBTQ rights and criminal justice reform—all from a unique Asian American perspective and experience.

This was a place where I could talk about my Asian American identity and growing up in an immigrant community. Where I met such legendary civil rights figures as Yuri Kochiyama, Grace Lee Boggs, and Philadelphia AIDS activist Kiyoshi Kuromiya. And where I cut my teeth on some of the biggest organizing campaigns that changed the course of Philadelphia politics.

When I arrived at AAU, they were already known for leading campaigns that reflected an intersectional and multiracial approach to the work: organizing immigrant tenants in West Philadelphia to win Section 8 housing; fighting a criminal justice system that went after Southeast Asian youth as gang members; tackling a struggling public education system with a lawsuit that won language access services for immigrant children; and working to save a public library in a diverse neighborhood in South Philadelphia.

I labored alongside working moms who brought their kids with them to community meetings. They were great artists and writers whose silk-screen posters delivered powerful messages that cut right to the heart of an issue. They gave inspirational speeches in front of hundreds of people. They took on the toughest issues, the biggest fights, and still figured out a path to win.

It took me a decade before I was ready to lead my first big campaign: the effort to save Chinatown from a billion-dollar, publicly financed baseball stadium being built on its borders. We organized a general strike with all the businesses in Chinatown. We ran a hard-charging media campaign. We shut down a major highway and rallied with community activists from across the city. And after months of organizing, we defeated the stadium proposal.

That was how I got my start in politics. While some people define political campaigns in terms of elections, candidates, and party alliances, my understanding of politics didn't start with politicians. It always started with a sense of "us." It started with organizing communities and building movements.

No movement was bigger than the movement for quality public schools in Philadelphia.

Just as my oldest daughter was getting ready to start kindergarten, the Commonwealth of Pennsylvania announced a hostile takeover of Philadelphia public schools. As a former teacher and a mother of three, I knew that the solutions to an underfunded, highly dysfunctional, and increasingly segregated public school system weren't going to come from superintendents, mayors, and our state legislators. Those solutions had to come from the people.

I joined a huge citywide coalition that brought out thousands of Philadelphians to oppose the state takeover and successfully limit privatization of the public schools. When that campaign ended, I went right back to work. We built school gardens and renovated school libraries. I worked with students to take on bullying and harassment in schools and with parents who volunteered their time to analyze school budgets.

The media weren't representing our voices, so I worked with organizers to start our own education newspaper. Too many elected officials were on the fence about school privatization and budget cuts, so I worked with researchers to get better data and information. When corporate education reformers unleashed multimillion-dollar advertising and lobbying campaigns to privatize schools, we trained one another on how to attend school board meetings and speak up with the messages that could win in the public sphere.

As the education justice movement grew, we merged with other broad-based movements for racial and social justice. Immigrant rights activists fighting for sanctuary cities. Criminal justice reformers working to end the school-to-prison pipeline. Housing advocates demanding resources to push back against substandard housing and homelessness. And a labor movement that stood up for workers—not just teachers and principals but maintenance workers and cafeteria workers, school crossing guards and police officers, who were often the lowest-paid workers in the system.

MY UNDERSTANDING OF POLITICS DIDN'T START WITH POLITICIANS

IT ALWAYS STARTED WITH A SENSE OF

★ "US" ★

For a long time, I was happy to stay outside the political system. I saw the power in the movements we were building, and I was perfectly happy to keep organizing and working to grow these movements.

I was fine with it, that is, until an anti–public education, union busting, privatizing, Republican governor took office and stripped funding from the state public education budget. We lost thousands of school staff, and the state takeover board rushed to close twenty-three public schools in one school board meeting.

I'll never forget that meeting. Inside, the boardroom was packed. Outside, hundreds of parents, educators, and students were gathered. Community leaders were outraged. The national teachers' union president, Randi Weingarten, came down and was arrested in an act of nonviolent civil disobedience.

In a matter of minutes, the state takeover body voted to close down nearly two dozen public schools.

That was one of the lowest moments I can remember in my work. But when the politics worked against us, I went back to that earliest lesson: This was about the political future we wanted, not the one we had. In that moment, I realized what I had helped build. We had the public on our side. We had a clear vision for the future. We had the power to mobilize. And now we needed to take that power and use it at the ballot box.

When our governor came up for reelection, I threw myself into his defeat. We made sure he remained the face of those budget cuts that had devastated school communities not only in Philadelphia but across the state. He became the first governor in modern Pennsylvania history not to win a second term in office.

The next year, the municipal elections in Philadelphia rolled around. We were electing a new mayor and voting for the whole city council. More than two dozen people had jumped in the race for the at-large seat on the city council. I was looking for a candidate to support, someone who would carry forward the education vision we had worked so hard to build. I waited and hoped for that ideal candidate. And then I realized that that person was me.

The decision to go from organizing to politics wasn't easy. I wasn't endorsed by the Democratic Party. I drew a terrible ballot position. And I had plenty of doors shut in my face.

At one of my very first public forums, the organizer opened with a scathing attack on public schools and talked about how public education had failed our children. Then he pointed to me to respond. I took a deep breath. I figured that if I couldn't talk to people about my vision, I probably shouldn't be running anyway. So I talked about what it meant to stand up in the face of dysfunction, failure, and injustice and to fight for kids. I won the room over. And I learned that's what politics, at its best, is all about: making what seems impossible possible.

Campaigning wasn't easy, but on so many levels I saw how it could be exhilarating to crisscross a city and talk about the issues you believe in, the people you love, and a vision that brings hope and investment. All the lessons I had learned over my twenty years of organizing kicked in—working small rooms and big rallies, reaching out to allies and coalition partners, meeting everyday people who could be the face of a new political future.

I could feel the momentum build as I knocked on doors and made endless phone calls. We raised more small-dollar donations than all but one of the mayoral candidates. And I had great partners in the local teachers' union and other educators.

In Philadelphia, where Democrats outnumber Republicans by a seven-to-one margin, the primary basically decides the election. So, on that May morning, I prepared myself for any outcome. I knew that I had done as much as I possibly could. I knew that I had led a campaign I could be proud of, win or lose. And I knew that throughout the city, no matter the outcome, a message of investment in our youth and our public institutions had resonated with voters like never before.

I won my primary. And that November, Philadelphians elected a mayor who embraced a strong pro–public education agenda, a judicial majority on the state Supreme Court who supported public school funding, and me: a daughter of immigrants, a first-time candidate, a woman, an outsider in almost every way.

Recently I met a mom who had just returned to the city as her daughter headed into public high school. She said Philadelphia's public education movement gave her hope.

"Keep fighting," she said. "This is bigger than all of us."

We, the people, built the political establishment and the political system we wanted and deserved. In some of our darkest times, political movements are born and built, and I will never stop fighting to keep that spirit alive.

ASHLEY BENNETT

Board of Chosen Freeholders // Atlantic County, New Jersey //
Elected in 2017

I WAS SET OFF BY A MEME.

"Will the Women's March be over in time for them to cook dinner?"

As millions of women marched in New Jersey, Washington, D.C., and all across the country, that's what a New Jersey freeholder posted on Facebook.

For me, that was the last straw. When I saw that meme, I knew that I could no longer be silent. I knew that I had to do something. I knew, deep down, that I had to run.

But service had been calling me long before that.

Shortly after September 11, 2001, I became an emergency medical technician. I planned to become a physician. But in the back of an ambulance, I realized the importance of quality mental health care, and I chose that as my career path instead. I studied psychology. And again, I had a realization: Mental health intersected with other issues, like the poverty and violence that plague some communities in New Jersey. So I went back to school and got graduate degrees in public health and business administration.

I wanted to help alleviate pain. All kinds of pain. And then the 2016 presidential election happened.

As an African American woman whose grandparents endured discrimination, I was proud to be a part of the generation that was moving us closer to equality for all. I was so excited when Barack Obama became the first African American to win the presidency. And I wanted to experience that shift again. I wanted Hillary Clinton to make history as the first woman to ascend to the country's highest office.

When she lost, I felt personally defeated.

I felt sad. I felt angry. I felt determined. I decided that if Hillary Clinton could put millions of cracks in that glass ceiling, I would make sure I did my part to take a sledgehammer to it. In a way, she passed the baton to my generation, and I felt like we had to run with it.

But that doesn't mean I ever considered running for office. It wasn't even a thought. I did decide to get more involved. I contacted my local Democratic Party and told them that I was interested in volunteering. When I heard about the Women's March that was being planned in Washington, D.C., I wanted to go, but I couldn't get time off work. So I watched from afar.

Even watching online and on TV was inspiring. Here was this sea of people—people who felt just like me, who wanted to do something proactive, who wanted to resist. Sign. Me. Up.

A few days after the Women's March, a friend called and told me to check my e-mail. I had a message from my local Democratic Party. In it, there was a screenshot of that meme.

I was shocked. And then angry. And that was before I realized the post was from my own local elected official!

After we lost in 2016, I took solace in the fact that New Jersey had voted for Barack Obama and Hillary Clinton. I thought that the misogynistic, racist rhetoric we heard from the campaign trail was coming from somewhere else. Far away from my community. Now here it was in my own backyard.

So I wrote to Freeholder John Carman. I outlined some of the challenges we were facing in Atlantic County. I ended my letter with a question: "With all that needs to be addressed, how do you have time to be on social media?"

I never heard back. I tried to tell myself that I had done my part. But I knew I could do more.

I agreed to go with my friend to the next freeholder meeting, where we would have a chance to address him directly. I was nervous. I took the day off of work, drove forty minutes in the rain, and mentally prepared myself. There were people lined up outside the door, which gave me some comfort. I thought I might not have to speak if there were others there to speak for me.

Two young women spoke. I was moved by their courage. They must have been in high school—one with tears rolling down her cheeks, the other's voice quivering with anxiety. I wondered if Carman realized how his actions had affected these young women. I asked myself, "Where is their role model? Where is their advocate?"

I had to say something. I mustered my courage and addressed the whole board about the meme. I waited to see how he would respond. I wanted to hear him apologize. I wanted him to say that he would do better. But instead he said it was a joke, that it wasn't his intent to offend anyone. He said that the women he surrounded himself with were "strong women" who weren't offended.

Well, in that moment, I was pretty damn offended. I thought about every time I'd been dismissed. Every time someone said my opinion didn't matter. And I thought about how other women must feel the same way.

I got up and walked out. But I wasn't alone. In an amazing sign of solidarity, the room cleared out. It was as if we all decided at the same time that we would no longer sit by quietly.

Later that night, I started to think about running against Freeholder Carman. I knew it was a long shot, but I talked with my family the next day. They didn't think it was a crazy idea at all. They supported me 1,000 percent. Not long after that, I announced my candidacy.

Working in health care, I often got a little frustrated. Helping one individual or family at a time is important, but to create systemic change it was clear that I needed to be engaged in policy and legislation. This was my chance to really help on the issues I cared about. This was my chance to alleviate pain in a new way, a critical way. And when I realized that, I knew I couldn't pass up this opportunity.

Now, running for office is hard. Don't let anyone tell you differently. It takes courage. When you put your name on the ballot, you're putting yourself in a vulnerable position. You're inviting criticism. So I get why most people want to avoid going through that.

I had a huge learning curve. But I just kept reminding myself why I got into the race: to help people. To bring them some relief. So, every time I doubted myself, I found the strength to keep running. I found that strength in my own determination. I found it in organizations that connected me with mentors and other candidates. I found it in my friends who rallied behind me and helped me craft a campaign message that spoke to our neighbors.

I was never the favorite to win, not even on Election Day. But I'm so glad I did. I'm so glad I saw that meme (as much as I hated it). I'm so glad I went to that meeting. I'm so glad I spoke up. I'm so glad I ran.

In response to that meme: The Women's March might not have been over in time for us to cook dinner, but it was over in time for us to run.

IT WAS AS IF
WE ALL DECIDED
★ ★ ★ ★ AT THE ★ ★ ★ ★
SAME TIME
THAT WE WOULD
NO LONGER
★ SIT BY ★
QUIETLY

ZACH WAHLS

State Senate // Iowa's 37th State Senate District // Elected in 2018

ON THE MORNING OF JANUARY 31, 2011, I woke up early, put on a suit and tie, and went to my engineering classes at the University of Iowa. I was nervous all day, struggling to focus in class, reviewing in my head over and over and over the words I had written the night before. After class, I got into my Pontiac Grand Am and drove to Des Moines as a light snow blanketed our state. I still remember going around the bend on the interstate and seeing the pale golden dome of the Iowa state capitol off in the distance.

When I walked into the capitol, I was overwhelmed by how many people had shown up. My only experience with legislative hearings was what I had seen on C-SPAN, which were mostly sleepy affairs. This was nothing like that. The energy in the Iowa House of Representatives was electric and unbridled. The chamber was filled with lawmakers, activists, and reporters—standing room only. My heart was racing. I didn't realize this was what I had signed up for.

The call had gone out for speakers about a week earlier. Iowa Republicans, riding the 2010 Tea Party wave, had retaken the lower chamber. They decided their top legislative priority was rolling back the unanimous Iowa Supreme Court ruling, *Varnum v. Brien*, recognizing marriage equality for same-sex couples, like my parents. As I read the e-mail about the hearing, I knew I had to go and speak for a simple reason.

My first homework assignment in the eighth grade was to watch speeches during the 2004 Republican National Convention. I was thirteen years old. I'll never forget what it was like to watch right-wing politicians stand up and warn our country about the dangers of terrorism and the Taliban and Al-Qaeda in one breath and warn of the threat of families like mine—of same-sex parents like mine—in the next. It was terrifying. I will never forget how it felt to think the government was coming for me and for my family. And I will never forget how it felt not to see anyone standing up for us. We felt so alone.

A few years later, I served as a volunteer young adult counselor for other children with same-sex parents. I looked into their eyes and told them it would get better, even though I wasn't sure how long it would take for that statement to become true. I heard same-sex parents talk with each other quietly, unaware the kids were listening, about their worries and anxieties.

As I read the e-mail about the hearing, I knew I had to go and speak because I knew that eighth-grade Zach would have been terribly disappointed in college sophomore Zach if I didn't go. I figured out what I wanted to say, and I drove to Des Moines, but I didn't have any idea what I was getting myself into.

The capitol was filled with strangers. Activists and the media and lawmakers and me, a young adult but really just a kid, waiting to see if they would call my name to speak. I didn't have any meaningful advocacy experience. I had never spoken about my family in public, and we hadn't been plaintiffs in the *Varnum* case. But I knew I was in the right place. I talked briefly in the lobby with some other children and their parents. We were all nervous. We all felt that our backs were up against the wall, and I was literally standing up against a wall because there was nowhere for me to sit.

I heard my name called. My heart was racing. I set my iPod Touch down on the desk behind which I was speaking, hit start on the timer, put my hands in my pockets because they were shaking, and said what I had to say.

The whole speech is online, if you'd like to watch it. But here's, I think, the most important part:

"The sense of family comes from the commitment we make to each other. To work through the hard times, so we can enjoy the good ones. It comes from the love that binds us. That's what makes a family. So what you're voting here isn't to change us. It's not to change our families. It's to change how the law views us, how the law treats us. You are voting for the first time in the history of our state to codify discrimination into the [Iowa] constitution."

When I was done, I went back to my spot against the wall and listened to the rest of the speeches. When the hearing was over, I started heading back to my car. I bumped into a woman I didn't know. Sue, a Democratic Party activist and former junior high teacher, had watched the hearing downstairs in an overflow room with two little boys who also had two moms. She sat with the family, holding their hands tightly. She thanked me for speaking up and for being there and told me what it was like to see the expression on the faces of those two boys as they watched someone stand up and fight for their family. She told me to never, ever stop fighting.

Seventy-two hours later, my life was turned upside down as the video of my speech went viral. It was gratifying at first, and I was overjoyed and enthused by all the praise my words received. But excitement gave way to fear as I realized the video and my words were taking on a life of their own that was beyond my control. Suddenly, I was everywhere, and requests—from the media, from advocacy groups, from other children with two moms or dads—were pouring in. And I had a choice to make: to keep my head down and focus on my engineering studies or to step up and keep fighting.

As I was weighing this choice, I got a call from my former American history teacher at West High, Mitch Gross. Mitch, a onetime political operative for the Democratic Party, told me he would have my back no matter what I chose, but that if I chose to keep fighting, he and his wife, Melanie, another former operative, would help guide me through the process.

I love my moms, but they work in medicine. "Going viral" means something totally different to them. And the support of Mitch and Melanie was exactly what I needed.

I spent seven years standing up for families like mine and people who have been left behind and left out. My advocacy in Iowa took me all over the state and then all over the country, to speak in towns and cities and on university campuses in defense of marriage equality and the inherent worth and dignity of all people. We held listening sessions in church basements and public libraries and at courthouses and house parties. The conversations weren't always fun or easy, but they always mattered.

In 2012, I cofounded an organization called Scouts for Equality, which was dedicated to overturning the Boy Scouts of America's decades-old ban on gay members and leaders. I'm an Eagle Scout. I grew up in the Boy Scouts, and the values I learned were that a Scout is trustworthy, loyal, helpful, friendly, courteous, kind, obedient, cheerful, thrifty, brave, clean, and reverent. Heterosexual was not on that list.

A group of us decided we would take on the Boy Scouts of America's ban on, in their words, "avowed homosexuals," which had been in place formally since 1978 and informally since the organization's founding in 1910. The Scouts had even survived a U.S. Supreme Court challenge in 2000, which meant they had about the strongest legal protection anyone can have, so we would need a different strategy.

We thought this would be an eight-to-ten-year campaign. And then, just six weeks after we launched in the summer of 2012, the Boy Scouts very publicly doubled down and said they would not change their policy. You might remember this, as it was headline news at the time. But growing up in the Scouts, I learned that you don't just give up because something is harder than you thought.

We kept at it. We mobilized hundreds of thousands of people to convince the Boy Scouts to do the right thing. And we got it done. Today, no Scout has to worry that he will be rejected because he is gay or transgender or that his family will be excluded or left out because he has two moms. Today, because of our work, the Boy Scouts of America respects and includes all American families.

Leading Scouts for Equality was, without question, the most difficult thing I've ever done in my life. Or at least it was until November 2017, when I got another phone call from Mitch. Our state senator was retiring. Mitch had thought seriously about running and decided the timing wasn't right for him and his family. Instead, he and Melanie thought I should run, and they wanted to help run my campaign.

After mulling over the decision, talking it over with family and friends, I knew the time was right for me to run. None of us will ever forget where we were on the night of November 8, 2016, or how we felt when we woke up on the morning of November 9 and realized that this was really happening.

Iowa has been ground zero for the change that we knew was coming at the state level. Republicans here rode our state's swing from President Obama to President Trump—which was the biggest of any state in the country—into full control of our state government. They wasted no time setting out to enact a right-wing agenda on health care, education, and workers' rights that is devastating communities like the one where I grew up.

And this feels personal, because when I think about community, I think about family. And I believe, as I said at the capitol, that what makes a family is our commitment to one another to work through the hard times so we can enjoy the good ones, that it comes from the love that binds us. That's what makes a family. And that's what makes a community. We've been through hard times. We're in a hard time right now. But we've had good times, too, and I know we will again. And when we do, our work is to make sure that we are all sharing in that prosperity. Because a lot of people are struggling and aren't sure if their kids are going to have a better life than they did. A lot of people feel left behind and left out.

I decided to run because I'll never forget how it felt to be excluded or how hard we had to fight to get a seat at the table. I decided to run so that I could fight for all Iowa families the same way I fought for mine.

SAIRA RAO

U.S. House of Representatives //
Colorado's 1st Congressional District // Candidate in 2017

MY LATE MOTHER IMMIGRATED to the United States because she couldn't get a job in India. Her name was Sybil Rao. We called her Greenie because she had a somewhat bizarre fascination with Alan Greenspan (another story altogether).

Greenie served our country for thirty-four years as a doctor at the Veterans Administration Hospital in Richmond, Virginia. She was stricken with rheumatoid arthritis, yet she still meticulously wrapped herself into a sari for work every day. I distinctly remember how she'd dip her swollen hands into hot wax, peel it off, and then fold, fold, fold.

This was the 1970s and 1980s. This was the capital of the Confederacy. There'd be days Greenie would come home from work and talk about the horribly racist and sexist things people would say to her. Usually of the "I'm not going to let a brown woman give me a checkup" sort. According to Greenie, she'd say something like, "OK, the next white male doctor can see you in six months. You'll be dead from butt cancer by then."

More often than not, these very patients became Greenie's close friends. One used to come by with bags filled with homegrown tomatoes, knowing they were her favorite.

Her stories ripped up my insides. From the earliest age I can remember, I worshipped my mother. Seeing her in physical pain was bad enough. But the racism and sexism she endured at work killed me. My sister and I would beg her to wear "normal clothes," as though shirts, pants, and suits could shield her from the bigotry.

She'd always have the same response. A big smile. And the next day, wax, peel, fold, fold, fold.

When I was in the fourth grade, the boy I was going with came up to me in the library and said, "I can't go with you anymore. My mom says I can't go with a black girl."

Greenie came home to me trying to rub the brown off my skin with a stone. I remember screaming, "This is *your* fault. I look like this because of you. Will you *please* stop dressing like that? You're making it worse."

She hugged me, smiled, and the next day: Sari Time.

The rheumatoid arthritis gave way to pulmonary fibrosis. Greenie died on June 4, 2012. Her funeral was on my thirty-eighth birthday.

Only recently have I realized what Greenie's sari was. It was her resistance. Her unwillingness to let go of her authentic self. Her inability to relinquish her core.

Around the same time I realized this about the sari, I noticed something about my own resistance: The Democratic Party establishment wasn't my ally. Namely, I'd been tokenized and used as a brown woman. The party wanted my money, my votes, my door knocks, but when it came time to talk about racism, refugees, or Black Lives Matter, these same representatives were silent, or worse. One told a brown friend of mine that civil rights wasn't one of her "issues."

For people of color, civil rights are a matter of life and death. So I wrote an article for the *Huffington Post*. It was called "I'm a Brown Woman Who's Breaking Up with the Democratic Party." The response was swift. The essay went viral, indicating I'd hit a nerve. People on one side "Bye, Felicia'd" me. Those were the party loyalists. Those on the other side applauded the piece, noting they, too, had felt left behind, lied to, taken for granted. They were white, brown, black, male, female, rich, poor. They said they had left the party and didn't plan to vote again. That freaked me out because, taken to the logical extreme, that would have been me and I couldn't conceive of a scenario in which I wouldn't vote. Finally, tons of people beckoned me to run for office, to challenge the status quo.

At first, I laughed. After all, I have two small children and have killed myself for six years building a company with a friend called In This Together Media. We produce diverse kids' books. Our company had finally taken off.

But then Christmas vacation of 2017 happened, and I couldn't sleep. I watched *Elf* on repeat, hoping for clarity. It dawned on me that what bothered me about the Democratic Party establishment was this: Career politicians in Congress with 100 percent safe seats weren't using their power and privilege to advocate for the disenfranchised. If I didn't use *my* power and privilege to challenge the status quo, I'd be just as bad. I either had to get into the ring—or shut up.

I thought of Greenie every minute. What would she do? It was clear what she'd do. I returned to Denver from my sister's house in Texas and filed with the Federal Election Commission to run for Congress as a Democrat.

I don't have an Indian accent. I couldn't fold myself into a sari to save my life. But I could run for office. I could fight for racial, social, and economic justice. My resistance would be being the change I wanted to see. For me, for my kids, for your kids.

Throughout my campaign, I was more pleasantly surprised, disappointed, sad, elated, angry, and peaceful than I've ever been in my life. Basically, how Greenie must have felt every single day. In moments of self-doubt, those times when I wondered whether I could carry on another day, ask for another dollar, give another speech, smile through the racism, the sexism, the hate, whether my heart could handle the love and the trust, I thought of Greenie. How much physical pain she was in. How much emotional pain she was in. How much she must have loved me and my sister to wrap herself in that sari each day. How much she adored her patients to forgive unkind words and welcome them into our home.

We are Democrats. We are Americans. We can and will do better. I know that in my heart, my mind, and my soul. This country was Greenie's country. This is my country. It's my kids'—and future grandkids'—country.

Greenie wore a sari so that I could run for Congress.

BARBARA LEE

U.S. House of Representatives //
California's 13th Congressional District // Elected in 1998

ON THE DAY SHE ANNOUNCED her historic candidacy for president, Congresswoman Shirley Chisholm said this:

"I am not the candidate of black America, although I am black and proud. I am not the candidate of the women's movement of this country, although I am a woman, and I am equally proud of that. I am the candidate of the people of America. And my presence before you now symbolizes a new era in American political history."

I first met Congresswoman Chisholm in California, not long after she gave that speech.

It was 1972. I was living in Oakland, attending college and raising two young boys as a single mother. I was running the Black Student Union at Mills College and volunteering as a community worker with the Black Panthers. Like most working moms, I was busy.

I was also a good student. Mills College, a women's college founded in 1852, demanded academic excellence. But that spring, I found myself on the verge of failing my government class. My professor required us, as part of the course, to do fieldwork on a presidential campaign.

At the time, the well-known candidates in the race were white men—Edmund Muskie, George McGovern, and Hubert Humphrey. I had little to nothing in common with these men, and I knew they had no understanding of my life or the lives of low-income women of color. So I refused to do the fieldwork, which made it certain that I would get an F in the class.

During that time—in my capacity as president of the Black Student Union—I invited Congresswoman Chisholm, the first black woman elected to Congress, to speak at the campus. To my surprise, she agreed.

Little did I know, Congresswoman Chisholm was also breaking new ground by running for president. She was in California to promote her pioneering campaign. For the most part, the media ignored her campaign. So I was shocked when I learned that she was the first woman to run for the Democratic Party nomination and the first African American to run for president of the United States.

Congresswoman Chisholm was the daughter of working-class immigrants who raised her to dream big for herself and the world. She was also a child of the Great Depression. She knew what it was like to live without. She wanted better for herself and her community.

In 1968, she was elected to serve her Brooklyn congressional district and became the first African American woman elected to Congress. And she did it her way. While other politicians were preoccupied by power, Congresswoman Chisholm fought for her constituents, day after day, to eliminate poverty, expand childcare, and ensure that all families could earn a living wage.

She knew that running for president would be her most defiant act. She was truly unbought and unbossed—a fiery, fierce woman who would not let anything stand in her way.

After she spoke at Mills, I introduced myself and told her I wanted to work for her. I admitted that I wasn't registered to vote—despite my passion for social justice, I believed the political system was rigged. I thought my vote wouldn't count. After all, Congresswoman Chisholm was the first politician I'd ever heard speak to my concerns.

She took me to task. She told me, "Little girl, you've got to register and get involved."

SHE WAS TRULY
UNBOUGHT
AND
UNBOSSED
A FIERY, FIERCE WOMAN
WHO WOULD NOT LET
ANYTHING
STAND IN HER WAY

I was a divorcée and a mother! An activist! No one called me "little girl." But she did.

I promised Congresswoman Chisholm I would register, and she asked me to join her campaign. The next few months opened my eyes to politics. While juggling my studies and raising my boys, I organized her campaign in Northern California right out of my Mills College government class. We took about 10 percent of the vote in Alameda County. And later that summer, I traveled to the Democratic National Convention in Miami and served as a delegate for Congresswoman Chisholm.

Although she lost the nomination, her run taught me the power of defiance. Those who told her not to run—that her campaign was impossible—were intimidated by her honesty and feared the kinds of changes her brand of political fearlessness could create.

She showed me that it was possible for women of color to seek change not just from the outside but also within our political system. And throughout her life, despite facing racism and sexism from people who did not believe she should be in Congress or run for our nation's highest office, Congresswoman Chisholm participated in the system so she could change it.

She used to say, "If they don't give you a seat at the table, bring a folding chair." And she lived by that principle.

Congresswoman Chisholm remained my lifelong friend and mentor. She taught me how to lift others while rising, to mentor other women and people of color along the way. Over the years, I have tried to apply the lessons of support and mentorship that she gave me to other women—and I have seen interns and staffers from my office go on to lead organizations, build grassroots movements, and become activists in their communities.

After her campaign, I spent the summer of 1974 in Washington, D.C., as an intern with a great warrior, Congressman Ron Dellums. That internship turned into a job, and I was one of only a few African American women running a Capitol Hill office.

When I ran for the California state assembly and state senate, Congresswoman Chisholm helped organize and build support for my candidacy. She counseled me through the stressful and exhausting election. During the victory celebration after I won my state senate seat, she said that she knew when she met me that I would one day be a member of Congress.

Her proclamation caught me off guard, but she told me that she could see potential where others could not.

Where some people saw a single mom struggling to make ends meet, Congresswoman Chisholm saw a future member of Congress. That was just who she was.

Her faith and confidence in me gave me the strength to believe in myself, too. And her guidance showed me how to run while being true to myself and my values, because an unapologetic and honest campaign would always be heard above scripted political noise.

I was heartbroken when we lost Congresswoman Chisholm in 2005. After her passing, I fought for a portrait of her to be hung in the U.S. Capitol. In 2008, I succeeded, and hers became the first and only portrait of a black woman in the Capitol—a trailblazer to the very end. I also led the effort to create a postage stamp for her. It took ten years, but we did it.

These were fitting honors for a woman who not only changed my life but also changed Congress. To this day, her strength and drive to challenge unjust laws and policies remind me to be persistent, do the right thing, and not let anybody turn me around.

I would not be where I am today without Congresswoman Chisholm and the many other women who came before me. They lived in our nation during a time rife with overt discrimination, segregation, and even racial violence—but these horrors only strengthened their resolve to create a better world. Their wisdom and guidance led me from a childhood of segregation to the halls of government.

Congresswoman Chisholm paved the way for me—and so many others—with her bravery and defiance in demanding that America listen to the voices of the people who were marginalized and shut out of the opportunity to seek the American dream. I stand on her shoulders. We all do.

Congresswoman Chisholm ushered in a new era of American political history. But that history is still being written. It's being written by the thousands of women and people of color and LGBTQ people who have stepped up to run for office. These candidates are fighting to change the country, just like the Honorable Shirley Chisholm did. They are speaking truth to power. And they won't let anything stand in their way.

I know Congresswoman Chisholm would be so proud.

DANIEL
HERNÁNDEZ JR.

Arizona House of Representatives // Arizona's 2nd House District //
Elected in 2016

I'M A TWENTY-EIGHT-YEAR-OLD openly gay Latino, born and raised in Arizona.

To say that I'm not a part of the establishment is an understatement.

Before I got involved in politics, my father hadn't voted in twenty years, because he felt the system was broken and that his vote didn't matter. And my mother was an immigrant from Mexico. She didn't become a citizen until 2016.

So running for office wasn't necessarily in the cards for me.

I had a wonderful grandmother who taught us grandkids a very important lesson: *"Pon tu granito de arena."* It means simply: "Put in your grain of sand." Regardless of who you are, or where you come from, we are all a part of something much bigger. We all have something to contribute.

From a very young age, this is what drove me.

One time, I was on my bed with my sisters Alma and Consuelo. I was five. Alma was three. She was jumping up and down on the bed and thought it would be funny to kick me.

WE ALL HAVE
SOMETHING
TO
CONTRIBUTE

I fell backward and hit my head on the metal filing cabinet that was next to the bed. I started bleeding. My sister started crying. And my mother came in to see a pool of blood and the three of us screaming at the top of our lungs.

My mother said we would have to go to the hospital. She put a towel around my head, and we sped off in a taxi. At that point, I'd only ever been to the hospital a few times to visit dying relatives.

My mother was so scared that she called ahead to let them know we were coming. By the time we arrived, a nurse was waiting outside for us. I tried to put on a brave face, but deep down I was terrified. I thought I was coming to die. Because, to me, then, that's what hospitals meant.

That nurse took me into her arms and said, "Sweetie, everything's gonna be OK." They did a quick evaluation of the cut and ordered some scans. The doctor then came in and put five stitches in the back of my head. He laughed and gave me a five-dollar bill and told me that I was getting a dollar for every stitch because I was being so brave.

He asked me if I wanted to see what he did for a living. He walked me around the emergency room and told people that I was his assistant. He gave me his stethoscope and asked patients if I could listen to their heartbeats.

These small moments of simple kindness changed the course of my life. I decided I needed to be a nurse or a doctor. I was going to put in my *granito de arena* and help people. I worked hard and trained as a nursing assistant and phlebotomist. By the time I graduated from high school, I was working at a local hospital.

With my sights set on medical school, I wanted to diversify my résumé. I had a lot of education but no real-world experience. I needed something to help me stand out.

I watched a video of the then senator Hillary Clinton announcing her first run for president and inviting people to help. I was interested. Within a few days, I got a job as an intern with her campaign and was working with a group of women who jokingly called themselves the "Yentas for Hillary." These women taught me everything—from how to knock on doors to how to build campaign events. Quickly I grew to love the work. It was thrilling to be part of something bigger than myself.

But then that campaign ended. I was disappointed. It was my first campaign, and we lost. I vowed to never work in politics again. I wanted to double down on my studies and become a doctor.

But a few days went by, and the "Yentas for Hillary" became the "Yentas for Gabby." Congresswoman Gabrielle Giffords was an incumbent in one of the most competitive congressional districts in the country. And although I was trying to leave politics behind, I accepted an invitation to one of Gabby's events.

It was electrifying. Gabby was young and dynamic, but, most important, she was real. As Gabby herself says, she doesn't do handshakes, she does hugs.

So I broke my own vow and again became an intern. I was precocious and scrappy. I was always around when needed and sometimes, I'm sure, even when I wasn't.

I was around so much, I became friends with Gabby. Eighteen years old and friends with a congresswoman.

I told her, the way I told everyone, that I wanted to be a doctor. But unlike everyone else, she didn't simply encourage me. She stopped and asked me, "Why?"

For Gabby, it was a passing moment. For me, that moment changed the course of my life forever.

I was taken aback by her question. She forced me to pause and think about it. And then I remembered what my grandmother had taught us.

When I told Gabby that, she asked if I'd thought about other ways to help people. She added that being a doctor wasn't the only way. I thought about it again. She was right.

Not too long after I started interning with Gabby, we were at a supermarket near Tucson, and nineteen people were shot. Gabby was one of them. Afterward, when people said I helped save her life, I was just glad I was there. I was just glad I hadn't quit politics. That I'd met her.

That was the beginning of 2011. By the end of the year, I was elected to the Sunnyside Unified School District governing board. I learned firsthand that what Gabby had said was true: There were lots of ways to make a difference. On the school board, we tackled everything from budgets to sex education.

Years later, I ran for a seat in the statehouse. Again, I won. And again, I saw how I could make a difference. My first bill, for instance, created additional protections for sexual-assault survivors. It passed with bipartisan support.

Running for office was never in the cards for me. Until I got involved. Until I met Gabby. Until she asked me that question. She put in her grain of sand. And for those of us who are underrepresented in elected office, those small actions can make a big difference.

HEATHER WARD

School Board // Pennsylvania's Tredyffrin/Easttown School District // Elected in 2017

DEAR ME ON NOVEMBER 8, 2016,

Today you are full of hope and excitement at the thought of our first woman president. Not just any woman, either. One of your sheroes.

You will remember the morning in preschool when you looked at a poster of all of our presidents and wondered where the women were. At four years old, you decided that you would be the first woman president. But today you will hope with all your heart that you will not, in fact, be the first woman president. Because today is the day Hillary Clinton is going to shatter that highest, hardest glass ceiling.

Tonight you'll have dinner with your friends. You'll scroll through Pantsuit Nation and talk about how amazing it will be to see the glass ceiling shattered. Look around at them. They will stick with you through it all. Be there for them, because they will be there for you. They are some of the most incredible women you will ever meet. They will make hundreds of phone calls for you. They will be your biggest cheerleaders.

Overnight, your worst fears will come true. Hillary Clinton will lose to the most mediocre white man on the planet. You will wake up scared and sad but mostly mad. You'll cry on the phone with your parents and later with your little sister. She'll tell you about all the kids who came to school that day crying because they were scared about the future of our country, about their future, and about their safety. Process it now, because you have a long year ahead of you. Don't forget those stories. Take all your fury and bundle it up to keep you going.

Your anger is going to lead you on the wildest ride you could possibly imagine. You will decide to channel that rage into running for school board. Why, might you ask, do you choose school board? Because that is where you can directly protect those kids in the district where you were born and raised, in the district your parents moved to so that you could have the best education. You'll run because every child after you deserves those same educational opportunities—whether or not the president and secretary of education believe in public schools.

You will start out pretty naive. Apparently there's a lot that goes into running for office, even at a local level. It will be OK. You'll learn. In a few months you'll laugh about having to look up what GOTV (get out the vote) stood for in the middle of a candidate training.

From gathering signatures on your petitions to raising money, designing campaign literature, running social media, and talking to thousands of voters, it will be so much harder than you could ever have imagined. Whenever you want to quit, remember that anger you felt on November 9. Remember all the kids who woke up scared and came to school crying. And then keep going.

I challenge you to introduce yourself to two new people at every event you go to. You are going to meet the most amazing, inspirational people during this journey. You will make new friends, building a campaign family as you go.

You'll knock on a lot of doors. At times you won't like it, but that's how you will win. On Election Day, people will tell you and your surrogates that they came to vote because you knocked on their door. They'll remember your name because you came to their door when it was 100 degrees outside or pouring rain.

You'll make a lot of phone calls. They're not any easier. But people will remember that you called them. One woman will vote because you called and made a voting plan with her.

You'll have to speak in front of hundreds of people and, no, that isn't any easier, either. But you'll get better at it as time goes on.

It will be exhausting. At times you will wonder whether this is all worth it. I promise you: it is.

People are going to slam the door on you. Negative mail is going to be sent about you. You will be doubted by many. Including yourself. You'll encounter sexism in ways you could never imagine. Keep going. Don't quit.

You'll also develop a network of people who will have your back. They will take your calls at all hours of the day and night. They will knock doors and phone bank and donate. One will call you from overseas to walk you through how to canvass effectively.

When you hear about a group called Run for Something, don't hesitate to apply. It seems ridiculous that they might care about your school board race, but they will become one of your most valuable resources. They'll open up a mentorship directory. The guy whose bio says he wants to talk about how knocking doors is the way to win? He actually does want to talk to you. Give him a call. You'll be glad you did. He'll be an amazing mentor, and knocking doors is the way to win.

During your final semester at Villanova University, you will miss out on parts of the college experience, and at times you will question your decision to run. Don't quit. This will be so much better than trivia night or tailgating before a basketball game. How many people can say they won a primary three days before graduating from college?

In his commencement address to your graduating class, Michael Bloomberg will say, "Patriotism is about how we respond when our founding values are tested." Don't ever forget waking up on November 9 and feeling like our founding values had been tested. Keep responding.

Sleep will become a luxury and caffeine a dependency (doesn't this make running sound like fun?). I promise, you'll be fine. But buy the good coffeepot for yourself. You'll use it.

Thank people constantly. You cannot do this without volunteers and donors. Make sure they know they are appreciated. You will have friends who are also running for office. Stand with one another, because you cannot do this alone.

When a woman running for coroner asks to canvass with you, say yes. (I know, it's crazy that coroner is an elected office.) Along with having a great time knocking doors with her, she'll help you with a paper for one of your classes. Ask the woman running for state representative if you can carpool to Washington, D.C., for a training. She'll answer your call on Election Day when you think you're going to fall apart. Take a leap of faith and ask the woman running for Congress out for coffee. She'll give you great advice and later knock doors for you during GOTV. (Now that you know what that stands for.)

At times you will feel like you are faking everything, and that's fine. You'll later find out that everyone feels that way. There will come a moment when you'll know what you're doing enough that others will ask for your advice. Stick it out until then.

Take breaks when you need to. That show *The West Wing*? You'll like it. *Pod Save America*? It's a good listen. Check out *The Riveters* while you're listening to podcasts.

It's OK to cry. You won't until the very end, but it would have been OK if you did sooner.

On Election Day, people will say, "Don't vote for the little girl." They will say you aren't good enough and you are a risk to our schools. Hold your head up high. Trust that you worked hard enough, that you knocked enough doors and made enough phone calls. Trust that the voters will show up.

When you collapse on your kitchen floor after polls close, when you have absolutely nothing left in you, know that you did everything you could have done. Know that you gave your heart and soul to this campaign, and that's all you can do. Trust that it will work out.

Before I go, I have a few last pieces of advice for you, Heather:

1. Don't ever forget why you are doing this. Don't ever forget those scared and crying children.

2. Ask for help when you need it. It turns out your cousin is a great graphic designer, one of your friends writes amazing speeches, and another friend is a master phone banker.

3. Stop worrying about what you wear; people will critique your outfit regardless. That's another fight for another day. If you want to wear bold red lipstick, then you should wear bold red lipstick.

4. No one has ever died from phone banking, and you won't be the first.

5. Every vote counts. That means you have to knock on the doors you don't want to. That means you have to finish every walk list even when you're tired. And, yes, that means you have to phone bank. (See number 4.)

6. Sleep whenever you can and wherever you can. (Except in class. Don't sleep in class.)

7. Chocolate solves almost every problem.

8. Call your parents. They can help solve the problems that chocolate cannot.

9. Say yes to everything. Even when you're scared. Especially when you're scared.

10. When people say you can't do something, do it anyway.

Tomorrow morning, your shero, Hillary Clinton, will say, "Never doubt that you are valuable and powerful and deserving of every opportunity in the world to pursue and achieve your own dreams." Take that to heart. You deserve everything that will come your way, because you will have worked incredibly hard for it. Don't let anyone tell you otherwise.

And remember, when all is said and done, when you win (yes, you win!), you get to shape the future of one of the top school districts in the country. Don't take that for granted. Being an elected official is an incredible honor and privilege. Enjoy every moment.

All My Love,
Me Today

SHEILA OLIVER

Lieutenant Governor // New Jersey // Elected in 2017

ON MY FIFTEENTH BIRTHDAY, in 1967, Newark erupted.

Unfortunately, it wasn't a birthday party. It was the third day of what we had come to call the Newark Rebellion. After years of seeing our city hollowed out, with jobs and opportunities going elsewhere, with issues of poverty, housing, and education going unaddressed by our leaders, residents had had enough. Over four days, many parts of my hometown burned or were looted.

The scars of the rebellion are still visible in the Newark of today—even after half a century, the city is still rebuilding. But one of the most lasting impacts is in the way it inspired a new generation of civic leaders. From the ashes of my city came new voices. I am one of them.

My eyes weren't opened to public service and the importance of an active, engaged, and responsive government—or the role I could play in it—overnight. I grew up amid activism. My uncles were involved in the labor movement. My neighborhood, a mix of African American and Jewish families, was always a place where community involvement ran deep. One cannot grow up in a place like that without a little bit of it rubbing off on you.

As an avid reader, I found my social conscience in the pages of *A Tale of Two Cities* and *The Grapes of Wrath*. Looking around, I saw their themes of social justice—of the haves and have-nots, of segregation and discrimination—played out in the streets of Newark.

In high school, I led a student walkout demanding that our voices be heard. We got a student appointed to the Newark Board of Education. I learned that government could change people's lives, but sometimes it needed to be pushed.

At Lincoln University, I was a member of just the third coed class in school history. I focused on my future as a social worker, taking my cues from classes in social institutions and history, realizing that—just as I did in Newark—I would have to fight for my place at the table.

Still, elected office wasn't in my plans or my thoughts.

I returned to Newark after graduation, working at a series of nonprofit organizations. I fought against exclusionary housing policies and to protect low-income housing from being demolished. I led the Newark Office of Youth Services and Special Projects, fighting for jobs for teenagers and for greater access to vocational education.

For the first time, I had direct access to elected officials who could help move the needle, including the pioneering state senator Wynona Lipman, the first African American woman ever to serve in New Jersey's state senate. And, for the first time, I began to think of the potential of serving in public office and being one of the decision-makers, as opposed to having to ask for a decision to be made.

By that time, I had left my hometown. But I didn't go very far, just to the neighboring community of East Orange. The mayor appointed me to the Board of Education, an experience that brought me right back to my early days fighting for representation in Newark.

In 1995, nearly thirty years after my hometown burned, I found my name on a ballot for the first time, running to serve as an Essex County freeholder—New Jersey's strange colonial-holdover term for county commissioners. I won that election and took my seat as one of five women on the nine-member board. I was selected as board vice president, and I never failed to challenge the president of the board, even though we were of the same party.

Two years later, I ran for mayor of East Orange, falling short by only fifty-one votes in the primary election. I decided not to run for reelection to the freeholder board in 1999, and I thought my career as an elected official was over. I returned to my nonprofit work, committed to making a difference.

In 2003, however, I was asked to once again run for office, this time on a ticket for the state legislature, as a candidate for the general assembly. To be honest, it was a post I didn't want and a campaign I didn't want to run, but I did it to support a dear friend and East Orange neighbor who was running for state senate and needed a complete slate. When the primary dust settled, he had lost, but I had won.

Ironically enough, without this election, I would never have become Speaker or lieutenant governor.

When I arrived in Trenton, I met with the incoming majority leader and my predecessor as Speaker, Assemblyman Joe Roberts. He said to me, "You have got to let me know what it is you want to focus on."

On my first day in the grand assembly chamber, I was embraced by the then assemblywoman Bonnie Watson Coleman—who would become the first African American woman to represent New Jersey in the U.S. House of Representatives. Her greeting to me was simple: "Welcome, sister. It's been awfully lonely here." I knew immediately where my focus would be.

I wanted to focus on creating change for women, for children, for marginalized populations, for African Americans, for immigrants, for LGBTQ New Jerseyans. I wanted to focus on the forgotten and the overlooked. I wanted to focus on the people who were left alone on the sidelines. I came to realize that I now had the bully pulpit to help the people who had looked to me for assistance throughout my career in social work.

I immersed myself in the rigors of the job. I rose to become chairwoman of the Assembly Human Services Committee, and I served on the Labor, Higher Education, Women and Children, Commerce and Economic Development, and Transportation and Independent Authorities committees. I grabbed a seat on assembly-senate joint committees on the public schools and economic justice and equal employment opportunity.

My colleagues rewarded me in 2009 by asking me to serve as Speaker of the general assembly for two legislative sessions, making me not only the first woman of color to hold the post in New Jersey but just the second in the nation to lead a legislative house (the first being California state representative Karen Bass, who has become a good friend).

In 2017, now-governor Phil Murphy asked me to join his ticket and become the first African American woman in New Jersey history to hold statewide office. Under our state constitution, as lieutenant governor, I could hold any post in state government—I chose to serve as commissioner of the Department of Community Affairs, returning to the issues of housing and community development through which I got my start.

I came full circle.

I worked hard to get here. But, make no mistake, from the path I had taken, I never bought into the appearances of politics. When I speak, it is my genuine feeling. And, when I fight, it is for the people I represent, not anyone who wanted to write me a check. Having to fight makes you a better legislator.

This is what we need more of in our politics. We cannot continue to dumb down our representation. We cannot forget that good politics stems from good public policy, and not the other way around.

We also cannot be lulled into thinking that if we just wish hard enough, the right candidate will someday come along. Oftentimes, that best candidate is ourselves. It takes a bit of bravado to put your name on a petition, but if no one else who excites you steps up to the plate, then it is up to you to do so.

Seeing more women putting their names on a ballot shows just how far we have come. I started in politics at a time when women were put on a ticket simply to draw votes for their running mates. I came up when the conventional wisdom was that women had an aversion to campaigning and raising money. Today, women are making themselves a presence in politics. Today, women are supporting other women.

One of my idols is the late New York congresswoman Shirley Chisholm, the first African American woman to serve in the United States Congress, who represented a district just across the Hudson River from my Newark home. She was as renowned for her fiery rhetoric as she was for her compassion. But she also serves as a model for public service, with the guidance, "You don't make progress by standing on the sidelines, whimpering and complaining. You make progress by implementing ideas."

When I was inaugurated as the lieutenant governor of New Jersey in January 2018, it was heralded as a historic moment for our state. Yet, as I said in my inaugural remarks, while we may make history in the moment, we ultimately write history with what we do with that moment.

It's not enough to talk about change unless you are willing to be part of that change. It's not enough to run for office unless you plan to do something with that office. Titles are nice. Progress is better.

DEBRA HAALAND

U.S. House of Representatives //
New Mexico's 1st Congressional District // Elected in 2018

MY MOTHER TELLS ME THAT I was born during a snowstorm. She had "gone home" to my grandparents in Winslow, Arizona, because the Marine Corps had shipped my dad off to a military base somewhere for a number of months. She thought it made sense to spend time with her parents. Having given birth to my two sisters, she knew when it was time to go to the hospital, and my grandpa drove her in the wee hours, his windshield wipers a-blazing.

My family is a military family. My mom and my siblings are also members of the Pueblo of Laguna. Assimilation policies played a large role in our lives.

My grandparents, like many Laguna families, moved to various parts of Arizona and California to work on the railroad. They raised my mom in a boxcar in Winslow, and my Laguna Pueblo grandmother, who was nothing short of a perfectionist, taught her every facet of our culture. My mom spent two years in the U.S. Navy and then twenty-five years as a federal employee, ensuring that Indian schools gained proper funding.

I inherited a tremendous work ethic from my mother and my grandmother, and I'm grateful for that. The beauty of working from the ground up is the experience you gain along the way. As your experience builds, it becomes easier to know how to instruct and, thus, lead. I never ask someone to do something I won't do myself. I lead by example. That's what they taught me.

While I was growing up, my mom would say our home was "well-kept." In reality, my siblings and I were spit polished, and the military shone through in every single floor tile and bed my dad could bounce a quarter on. We never argued. We just did as we were told. We learned discipline. We learned to grow a thick skin, and in moving so much and attending so many schools, we learned resilience.

All that was important, but still, by the time I reached middle school, I realized that I preferred to approach things in a more relaxed manner. I didn't feel comfortable dictating, as my mom did, and I felt I could accomplish what I wanted to in my own way.

I had some mentors who supported me in that. Ed Zinn, who owned a local bakery in Albuquerque, gave me my first job. I started as a salesgirl, walking to my part-time job every day after school. After about a year on the job, I was promoted and managed the part-time shift, ensuring that we all lived up to Zinn's reputation as the best bakery in town. Eventually, Ed's wife, Karen, was so impressed with my ability to learn quickly, she moved me to the cake-decorating department—which meant more hours and a pay raise.

Ed and Karen led by example. After I graduated from high school and started working full-time, I'd arrive at work at six in the morning. Often, the two of them were there when I arrived and continued to work long after I was gone. I learned how to work hard and fast, how to make my steps count. I also built up my muscles, because lifting large trays of cookies and cakes will do that to you.

I finished my thirteen-year bakery career, and I started college. I was twenty-eight years old. It was there that I began to lead. When I was passionate and put forth the effort, I found that I could gain the support of others to help me accomplish my goals.

During my sophomore year at the University of New Mexico (UNM), I organized a lecture by renowned Hawaiian activist Haunani-Kay Trask. I approached every single department head asking for the money to bring her to UNM. She came and gave a heartfelt lecture on the history and status of Native Hawaiians—how their queen was imprisoned and how the tourist trade was detrimental to the economic success of many Native Hawaiians. I was proud that I had created an opportunity for my community to learn about Haunani-Kay and her culture.

During law school, I pushed to get a bill passed that gave in-state tuition to Native American students, regardless of their residency. I was able to show state legislators that Native Americans never lose their residency with their own tribal communities, regardless of where they live, and I was able to get my fellow classmates and professors to drive to Santa Fe for committee hearings to support my bill. I also started working to get Native voters registered and to the polls.

After I graduated from law school, I knew that I wanted to continue to lead and to serve. I wanted to be like my mother and my grandmother. They worked hard and found ways to help people. They showed up.

I've run for office three times. In 2014, I ran for lieutenant governor in New Mexico. I felt my party needed a candidate who could bring something different to the table. I'd spent years in Indian Country, and I thought I could inspire that demographic to get out to vote. I won the Democratic Party's nomination, but in the general election our strong platform on education and equity for working people was no match for the incumbent governor's massive war chest.

That year we lost our statehouse, too. Morale was low, but I remained undeterred. I felt I could still offer some fresh energy to our party, so I traveled the state talking to Democrats about my vision—to be united and work hard to win. I ran and became the first Native woman state party chair in the country. After I won, I met with fellow Democrats, across the state, every chance I got.

When my term was near its end, the congressional seat in my district opened up. I asked myself whether I could run a winning campaign. Could I gather a winning team I trusted and who trusted me? Could we work hard enough? Could we amass the support to raise the funds needed to run a compelling, relevant, and professional campaign that could touch voters and turn them out to vote?

The answer to every question was yes.

I wanted to make the case for renewable energy in my state. I wanted to make the case for public education. I wanted to make the case for strengthening communities, especially underrepresented communities like the one I grew up in.

So I launched my run for Congress, and I promised myself that I'd run an inclusive campaign—in terms of whom I hired and which voters we were trying to reach. And I committed to working as hard as my staff and volunteers.

When I think back on how and why my life turned out the way it has, I have to give all the credit to my family, to my mentors, to my role models, especially the strong women like my grandmother, my mother, and Karen Zinn. And the women who have made history—Shirley Chisholm, Dolores Huerta, and Elizabeth Warren. These women have dared to show up, to step up, and to lead, and they continue to inspire me.

Whether in person or through the pages of a book, these women have shown me that leadership means being consistent—maintaining the right attitude and sense of resolve. Leadership means never being satisfied with how things are but always striving to make things better, because the people you stand with on the front lines deserve that.

And I'll continue to lead no matter what.

LEADERSHIP
MEANS NEVER BEING
SATISFIED
WITH
HOW THINGS ARE
BUT ALWAYS STRIVING
TO MAKE THINGS
BETTER

VALERIE HEFNER

House of Representatives // Texas's 62nd House District //
Candidate in 2018

MY DAUGHTER, ARRIANNA, IS TRANSGENDER.

At school, she was singled out every day. She was forced to go to the
nurse's office anytime she had to use the bathroom. Each time she got the
pass to go, suspicions were raised. Questions followed her everywhere. She
would come home and cry. "Why do I have to be a trans girl?" she'd ask.
"Why can't I just be a girl?"

I held her as she cried. I tried my best to build her up.

When the Obama administration issued new guidelines that said that
transgender students have the right, under Title IX, to use their preferred
bathroom in public schools, everything changed for us.

"No student should ever have to go through the experience of feeling
unwelcome at school or on a college campus," John King Jr., the secretary
of education, said when the guidelines were released.

Amen. Things were finally going to get better.

That was May 13, 2016. On August 22, 2016, which was Arrianna's
first day of the new school year, I woke up to the news that U.S. District
Judge Reed O'Connor, a federal judge in Texas, was blocking the executive order.

It was frustrating and heartbreaking. I tried to get answers from the school district, but no one knew what to do. I couldn't bear to tell my daughter the whole of it. I just told her to use the girls' restroom and that I would deal with it.

At the very least, I figured that with a new president—a new, progressive, female president who stood with LGBTQ Americans—my daughter would not be forgotten, and this would all get sorted out again.

Then came November 8, 2016.

I was so excited. I came home from work and turned on every TV in the house. I made dinner. I wanted my kids to remember this day for the rest of their lives. We were witnessing history. And once Hillary Clinton was elected, they would know that anyone could be president. No matter what.

Then the map started to turn red, then redder. I had this slow, sinking feeling in my stomach. I sat on the couch, numb, on the verge of tears. My husband sat holding my hand on one side; Arrianna was asleep on the other side. At one point, she stirred, looked up at me with sleepy eyes, and said, "Did she win, Mama?"

I woke up early the next morning. We went about our morning routine. Quieter than normal. When I got to work and saw my colleagues crying, I cried, too.

The new administration started out exactly as I had feared.

On February 22, 2017, Donald Trump rescinded the Obama administration guidelines that had given my family so much hope. Then there was the Muslim ban and the rise of neo-Nazi violence. Then there were attacks on journalists and judges and immigrants. It felt like a bad dream that we couldn't wake up from. Still does sometimes.

I'm a true 1990s punk kid at heart. In those early days of the Trump administration, Green Day, one of my favorite bands, gave me hope. They put out a single just a few days before the inauguration called "Troubled Times." The song goes:

> What part of history we learned
> When it's repeated
> Some things will never overcome

If we don't seek it
The world stops turning
Paradise burning
So don't think twice
We live in troubled times

On March 4, 2017, Green Day was scheduled to play in Dallas. I just had to go. For my sanity. I needed to be in a room full of like-minded punks and purge some of the negative energy that was boiling up inside me. I sang. I danced. When Billie Joe Armstrong screamed, "Fuck you, Donald Trump!" I screamed right along with him.

There's a picture that was snapped at the end of the concert of me and my husband. You can see the relief on my face.

So I decided that was how I was going to get through the Trump administration: surround myself with like-minded people and get involved.

I started by picking up the phone. I called every one of my representatives to tell them my story and ask if they could help my daughter. I didn't feel like they heard me. My state representative didn't call me back. Our lieutenant governor had a weird obsession with bathrooms. And our governor wasn't reining him in.

I realized we had to vote different people into office.

I heard that Beto O'Rourke was taking on Ted Cruz in the race for the U.S. Senate. Beto was speaking in Allen, Texas, on May 19, 2017. I decided to go. There were hundreds packed into a brewery to hear him. Beto came out and captivated the audience and made it seem like the impossible—taking on an incumbent senator rolling in PAC money—was possible. After he spoke, he stayed behind and talked with every single person.

When it was my turn, I took a selfie with him. I told him what was going on with Arrianna. I cried. I actually cried and begged for his help. He looked at me and said, "I promise that I am doing my best to win this thing. And if I do, I promise to do everything in my power to protect your daughter."

During the state legislative session that year, there were a number of bills that would have made things worse for my daughter, that would have put a target on her back. Parents I knew from a local support group, DFW

Trans Kids and Families, rushed to Austin to testify against them. The bills flew through the House and just barely got stopped in the Senate.

During the special legislative session, more of the same bills were being pushed. I listened to hours and hours of testimony from parents, kids, members of the clergy, educators, and physicians who spoke out against these bills. In the end, we were saved by an unlikely ally. Joe Straus, Speaker of the Texas House, basically sacrificed his job to protect transgender children. He successfully blocked the so-called bathroom bill.

At some point in the middle of all this, I found myself at a gathering at a Panera Bread being hosted by the Democratic Women of Grayson County. I figured it was another chance to surround myself with people who thought like me and a good opportunity to get involved. I was so intimidated once I got there that I almost left. But I mustered my courage and joined the group.

All the women there seemed as excited to meet me as I was to meet them. We exchanged some small talk and I introduced myself. I explained that I needed to be around people who felt the way I did. I told them I felt smothered by everything that was going on in Austin with the bills and in Washington with the chaos. I said that it felt as if no one could hear me, that no one really understood what my family was going through.

One of the women there, Pamela McGraw, a local defense lawyer, asked me, "Have you ever thought about running for state representative?"

I responded, "No, I have never thought about running myself. I just keep hoping that someone else will."

Then she said, "Well, why not you?"

I didn't have a good answer. The meeting ended. We finished our coffees and parted ways. But those questions stuck with me.

I couldn't stop thinking about what she'd said. I lay in bed that night and thought about how it seemed like the last year and a half had been leading up to this very moment. It seemed like the universe was preparing me and pushing me in this direction. I was scared. Reluctant. But then a memory hit me like a ton of bricks.

"I'm so scared, Mama."

That's what Arrianna had told me on her first day of fifth grade, the first time that anyone at school would meet her as her true self. She held my hand and looked at the ground. She was trembling. I stopped. I put my finger under her chin and pushed it up so our eyes met.

I told her, "Lift your chin up. Never look down to your feet in shame. This is who you are, and you have no reason to be ashamed. I know you are scared, but you can do this because you are also strong. You are brave."

She must have believed me, because she took a deep breath, squared her shoulders, pushed her chin up, and walked through those doors.

And when I remembered that moment, I knew I had to do it. I knew I had to be brave. So I took a deep breath and pushed my chin up and decided to run.

MICHELLE LUJAN GRISHAM

Interviewed by Stephanie Schriock

Governor // New Mexico // Elected in 2018

STEPHANIE SCHRIOCK: You come from a family that has already broken through some pretty big barriers in New Mexico, including your grandfather being the first Hispanic chief justice of the New Mexico Supreme Court. I wanted to hear a little bit about your family history and their engagement in public service.

MICHELLE LUJAN GRISHAM: One thing about that: I had no real sense of it until I was an adult navigating my own path, which is really interesting, because they make a joke in Washington, D.C., that there are three political parties: Republicans, Democrats, and Lujans. I never really had a feel for politics until I had my own public career, but my family's involvement began even before my grandfather. My great-grandfather, a fellow by the name of Mateo Lujan, was the largest sheep rancher in New Mexico in a remote northern county. He was part of the original state constitutional convention, wherein they wrote the legislation for New Mexico to be a state. He was with President Taft when Congress passed the legislation and the president signed that legislation and New Mexico became a state.

SCHRIOCK: That's amazing. So, your great-grandfather is a founding father of the state of New Mexico?

LUJAN GRISHAM: That's exactly right, and then his son became the first Hispanic New Mexico Supreme Court justice. And then, chief justice.

SCHRIOCK: That's extraordinary. But you said something interesting. You didn't really know this history until you started getting politically involved yourself. Did the family not talk about it?

LUJAN GRISHAM: They didn't talk about it, and my grandfather, the New Mexico Supreme Court justice, retired the year I was born, so to me he was just an older guy. Evidently when my father was on his way to law school, my grandfather told him, "No, no, no! No more lawyers. No more politics. You're going to dental school." So my dad didn't even get to pick his career. My grandfather sent him to Creighton University to be a dentist. My father was a great dentist, but he didn't allow that career choice to prevent him from doing public service.

My dad ran a couple of great local Democratic races, and he was the first public-health dentist in the state. Even in this campaign, I talk about my dad having a dental chair in the garage in our first house in Santa Fe, because he did dental work for free for people who couldn't afford the care, primarily disabled children. He even paid for people's lab work. He just did it all.

My mom took on every other public institution that wasn't doing the right thing by disabled kids in New Mexico, but I got to live this incredibly normal childhood that was fun and loving without ever really recognizing how my parents were impacting their community and their state. Of course in my dad's day there was no social media, really—you just had newspapers. And for my grandfather to run for the Supreme Court, he had to be a DA in ten little communities. So my family would move to a little county or a little city, and my grandfather would run for DA, get elected, and do that for a couple of years, and then he'd move to another community to run for DA, and that's how you built a statewide race.

SCHRIOCK: Oh, my goodness.

LUJAN GRISHAM: And then another set of Lujans were incredibly successful politicians and still are in the state. They're all Republicans.

SCHRIOCK: What's interesting, though, is that even though politics per se wasn't talked about, you were sort of schooled as a child to make a difference. So, what was the moment in your life when you decided to step up and make a difference?

LUJAN GRISHAM: I fell into a job in 1987—it was one of those perfect storms. I didn't know what I wanted to be when I grew up. I'm out of law school. I'm working at a big firm, and it's not the right job for me. I fall into this program that serves senior citizens—it's called Lawyer Referral for the Elderly Program—and I start to listen to people's problems. Immediately, I recognized that, "Oh, my gosh. This is exactly what I watched my parents do all day long," and it certainly meant something to their community. I was all in. I wanted that job and wanted to make that difference for seniors. It catapulted me into a public service career.

SCHRIOCK: Then when did you decide that electoral office was going to be the next step?

LUJAN GRISHAM: When I listened to Hillary Clinton and Barack Obama, in their 2008 primary election, talk about health care and that the federal government had to do something about changing the United States' health-care system. I had been fighting the Feds and piecemealing together long-term health care for New Mexicans, and I wanted to be part of that bigger picture. I thought it was the most exciting shift in Democratic leadership for a policy that would—and still is going to—make or break where we are as a democracy in this world by making sure health care is a right and not a privilege. I wanted in.

SCHRIOCK: You had been doing some health-care work. By this point, had you done that undercover situation in the nursing home? Do you want to talk a little bit about that and how you found the courage to do something like that?

LUJAN GRISHAM: I guess I take after my mom and my dad. When they couldn't change something, you know, they just took it over. I was the cabinet secretary for aging; the department advocates for vulnerable disabled adults and seniors, though I had no regulatory authority. I was finding these horrific examples of abuse and neglect and exploitation—horrific. Where call buttons to summon help were taped under residents' beds so they couldn't call for assistance. People were physically abused; eighty-year-olds were raped. Men and women were dehydrated and malnourished so that they didn't have to be toileted. It was just the most horrific set of circumstances I had ever seen in my life. We were complaining and reporting these abuses to the regulators in state government, but nothing ever happened. I had just had enough, so we went undercover. I did it with another lawyer, and New Mexico is still the only state in the country that does anonymous care evaluations. I stayed three days in a long-term care facility, posing as a disabled woman who'd had a severe stroke during childbirth: Allegedly I was paralyzed and unable to take care of myself. My husband was divorcing me and had taken the newborn baby, and I was supposedly left in my father's care. He just brought me to a facility with two hundred dollars cash and no contact information or medical records, and they took me.

SCHRIOCK: Wow. They took you, and then what happened?

LUJAN GRISHAM: I did not suffer any significant traumatic injuries—I was lucky. But I didn't get toileted for six and a half or seven hours—I had to wet the bed. I was bathed by a twentysomething-year-old who did not know how to do it. It was incredibly humiliating. Then they couldn't dress me, because I was paralyzed, so they just wrapped me up partially in a towel and left me, wet and naked, sitting on a couch in front of all the guests and all the other residents for hours. I watched them humiliate and berate older residents who were looking for their mail or who wanted to make phone calls that they prohibited them from. I listened to them tell the family of a significantly behaviorally challenged geriatric patient, whom they were not qualified to care for, that they could take him. They would bring me my food, but I couldn't reach it or hold it because I was paralyzed, and when I didn't eat it, they just threw it all away. I didn't get my meds—my dad had made up a bunch of meds that were basically inert—and they weren't timely with pain medications for the other residents. And when I snuck away, they lied to my father, who was pretending to check on me, and said I was sleeping when I had already left the facility. They stole everything I came in with—all of it fake, including a fake diamond ring.

SCHRIOCK: That's extraordinary.

LUJAN GRISHAM: And then we shut them down. Three days after I exposed them, they lost their license. Their other facilities were also shut down, and residents were transferred to quality programs. We changed the regulatory framework in the state, and we're leading in the country for improving the quality of care for long-term nursing-home residents.

SCHRIOCK: That's such an extraordinary story. Of course, you probably broke your grandfather's heart by going to law school—he thought he'd broken the pattern with his son, the dentist, and then you go to law school.

LUJAN GRISHAM: He was still alive, but he wanted me to go to law school; he was over it by then! He was excited that I went to law school.

SCHRIOCK: You go undercover to change your state's health-care system, and you hear the 2008 presidential candidates talking about health care. When did you decide you were going to run for Congress in 2008?

LUJAN GRISHAM: September of 2007. I had no idea what I was doing and did exactly what you should not do. I had my best friend, who also thought he had a great idea, and the two of us sat at the kitchen table reading online how you file to be a candidate for Congress. I had no idea about any of the political issues you have to at least be aware of. I thought it was just about vision and wanting to make a difference and being able to articulate what some of the tougher issues are. I didn't understand name recognition and had no idea how to fund-raise. I didn't understand the complexity of running in a federal race. I had no idea about field or, when you get close enough, how to do GOTV (get out the vote). I didn't know how to hire campaign folks, and I was lucky enough to get connected to EMILY's List, so thank you, Stephanie. While I didn't have a mature campaign, so I couldn't win an endorsement, I didn't actually deserve one. We weren't going to win that race, and we weren't willing to do the things to try to get close. There was also another female candidate making many of the same mistakes I was, so it was not a good race for EMILY's List in 2007 and 2008. But losing that race taught me more about how to win and what I needed, and it didn't scare me away from wanting to make a difference and get elected. It motivated me to keep trying.

SCHRIOCK: We all made up for it the next go-round. Was that 2012?

LUJAN GRISHAM: That was 2012, but you stuck with me—something that is really important for what this book is about: organizations like EMILY's List. When I ran in 2010 for the county commission, because now I had the name recognition, I knew how to do a political operation, and I was a little bit better at fund-raising. I'm a little late. I jump in there late, and while it's not a race EMILY's List gets involved in, I still had access to the tools and resources and training and experience and the people I'd met there. So I kept those connections, and they made the kind of impact that you need. I was the underdog in the 2010 commission race and won it, and then Representative Martin Heinrich ran for the U.S. Senate, so in 2012, I ran for the seat I had originally lost.

SCHRIOCK: And you were an awesome candidate.

LUJAN GRISHAM: I was a good candidate, but I still needed a little coaching and a little advice.

SCHRIOCK: You know, if we're not learning in all of our jobs, we're not doing the right thing. Now you are poised to be the first Democratic woman of color to serve as governor in this entire country. Growing up the way you did, did you ever imagine this moment to be this close?

LUJAN GRISHAM: No, and I wonder how many experiences are just like mine, primarily for women. I think there are a lot of men who are good, qualified candidates and elected officials who can visualize seeking and winning public office early in their lives and careers. I never had any such idea. You know, I loved consumer protection, but I really never thought about running for office until that 2008 opportunity. I never thought about what the rest of that trajectory would look like. Now I get to come back home to a state I love and help Democrats all across the country make sure we get redistricting and other issues like health care right for our constituents. I am really excited about this opportunity, and I am really motivated to make a difference.

SCHRIOCK: That's so good. What's really interesting about you and so many of the women who have run is that you lost a race and that you came back. What did you gain from the experience of losing, and do you feel that made you better at what you're doing now?

LUJAN GRISHAM: When I give speeches to organizations like Emerge America that are intended to inspire and motivate women to run for office, I invariably meet someone who will say, "I don't think I can ask someone for money." And I say, "Of course you can. People want to help you succeed and make a difference, and they know what you need in order to do that." You just have to keep that in the back of your mind.

Campaigns are awful. Running for office is heinous, mean, unfair, grueling, exhausting, and demeaning. And even though I understand that people are willing to help me with their personal resources to make a difference, I don't want to ask them. I'd rather have a hot, flaming poker in my eye than start call time, but I will. It's really terrible, and somehow, even if you lose at the end of it—and that's what is important about losing—you learn about what you need to do strategically. You learn how to not make the same mistakes.

But you also learn that it's worth it—every bit of it is worth it—because these goals that the women are running for to make a difference are worth it. Every time I'm on the campaign trail and someone says, you spoke to me about this, and now I'm volunteering and mentoring youth in my community; or, you made a difference and saved my house; or, I didn't even know there was support for my disabled child until I read you did this or heard about this vote—everywhere you go, people are impacted by your efforts, and they want to help you and want to engage. That's how you build a community and a nation that is making a difference. It's always worth it, even in those darkest moments when you're being attacked. So you learn both those things from a loss. I don't think anyone feels lucky about losing, but that was the race for me to lose, because maybe I wouldn't be running for governor if I had won that race.

SCHRIOCK: That's so true. I have one last question. Last week, we saw Supreme Court decisions that were depressing, we learned more about the immigration crisis, which is depressing, and we heard about the retirement of Justice Kennedy, also depressing. What keeps you grounded and committed through all of this?

LUJAN GRISHAM: Two things. I always get a sense that those folks who are making these kinds of decisions—I mean, anybody who would separate children from their parents and even think about creating a "facility," a "tender facility," for toddlers—there's just something so heinous and evil and wrong and so misguided about an administration that would think about that and then launch it. I'm still horrified, and knowing that there are such people out there and knowing what the Supreme Court can do to my granddaughter, I am more motivated than ever that states have women who are running for office in every single place, from school board to governor and U.S. Senate and president. We have to regain our moral compass and conscience, and we have to stand against this newfound evil that is, I think, intended to minimize fairness and equity and equality in this country. Left unchecked, it will destroy our democracy. I see women standing up all across the country at all levels, and this is how we fix it. And fix it, we will.

SCHRIOCK: That was awesome.

LUJAN GRISHAM: It's so true. But I have my dark moments; I can't even watch *The Handmaid's Tale*, because it scares me. We're living it, but I'm going to fight against it. We all are, and people are unifying. Even in my own community, I'm seeing people stand up, rise up, and say things they might have been quiet about a decade ago, but they aren't now.

SCHRIOCK: It's so true. Do you still have your puppy?

LUJAN GRISHAM: I still have my puppy, Kiwi, and she's getting pretty fragile and old, but she's still with me, that dog. That's still the best press I got in my life—when Kiwi was found and returned to me—honestly. She was gone thirteen months, and I was destroyed. I launched a campaign to find her. With canvassers and ads, I did robocalls, Facebook, hired a dog detective, talked to consultants.

SCHRIOCK: Where had Kiwi gone?

LUJAN GRISHAM: She'd run away because a balloon scared her. I think someone just saw her in a high-traffic area and put her in the car and never got her chip checked. They just kept her until she ran away from them. Whoever had her didn't have the resources to take very good care of her. I'm glad she was returned to me, because she now has a more expensive dental program than I do.

SCHRIOCK: At least you come from a family of at least one dentist.

LUJAN GRISHAM: Right, professional courtesy.

This interview has been edited for length and clarity.
Stephanie Schriock is the president of EMILY's List, which endorsed Governor Lujan Grisham.

JASON KANDER

U.S. Senate // Missouri // Candidate in 2016

I DECIDED I DIDN'T WANT a concession speech.

It wasn't out of arrogance. It wasn't that I thought it was bad luck. It wasn't that we ran out of time. My campaign team and I decided we liked the victory speech so much that I'd just figure out what to do if I didn't get the chance to use it.

So when I walked onstage to concede my race against Senator Roy Blunt after a hard-fought, twenty-one-month campaign that started off with people giving me no chance and ended up as one of the highest-profile races in the country, I winged it.

Going back a few hours, we were feeling pretty good. Our internal polling and public polls showed the race as a toss-up. And shortly after the polls closed on November 8, 2016, exit polling had us up by a lot—one had the gap around seven points.

In Missouri, votes from Democratic-leaning areas tend to come in after 10:30 P.M., so I knew I'd be trailing most of the night, and it was going to be a long time until we knew if we won. The mood at our election night party in Kansas City was cautiously optimistic.

Then results from the presidential race started coming in. Too many states were "too close to call" in a race most of us didn't think would be close. Then before 9:30, Ohio was called for Donald Trump. At 10:07, it was North Carolina. At 10:30, it was Florida.

At that point, I was devastated for the country, because it was pretty clear Donald Trump was going to be elected our next president. I hadn't even considered that a possibility, so I was shocked. But the numbers in my race were still OK. We were hanging on.

In 2012, President Barack Obama lost Missouri by 10 points, and on the same day (and same ballot) I became the first millennial in the country to win a statewide election, winning the secretary of state's race by 1.5 points. In 2016, my campaign team figured out I could win even if the worst-case scenario occurred and the Democratic presidential ticket lost Missouri by as many as 15 points.

It turns out they were right in their calculations but wrong about what constituted the worst-case scenario, because Donald Trump ended up winning Missouri by 19 points. I lost by fewer than 3, so we over-performed the top of the ticket by 16 points. About 220,000 people who voted for Donald Trump for president also voted for me for the United States Senate, more than anyone in a competitive race in the country, but I still lost.

So there I was, about to go onstage to give a concession speech for the first time in my life—I had won my previous three elections, two of which were major surprises to the Missouri political world.

When I walked up to the podium, my victory speech was still on the teleprompter. Not a great start. With no script, I just let fly what was on my mind, and in that moment my biggest fear was that something as heart-breaking as a Donald Trump presidency might chase my own generation out of politics permanently.

I wanted to use my platform to talk to them. I looked out at my supporters, and I said:

"[This generation needs] to know that I'm not OK with them stepping away. That this country is a place that you've got to stay invested in. You don't get to decide that you are going to be OK with the politics, that you're going to believe in the politics of this country when it goes your way. That's not how it works in this country."

The next day, there was an article in the *Christian Science Monitor* headlined "Who Is Jason Kander, and Why Is His Concession Speech

Drawing Attention?" The St. Louis CBS affiliate wrote, "Kander Gives Passionate Concession Speech, Tells Generation to Not 'Check Out.'"

If I was going to challenge my generation to stay engaged, I knew I needed to do it with more than just talk. I had been granted a national voice, and I needed to figure out how to use it, since it wasn't going to be as a United States senator.

But I hadn't always had that platform. When I started my campaign, nobody gave me a chance. I was a thirty-three-year-old progressive Democrat who had been arguing for single-payer health care since 2009, was a vocal supporter of Planned Parenthood, and had an F rating from the NRA. Reporters and political pundits tried to figure out what I was thinking by giving up a relatively safe reelection campaign to take on one of the most entrenched politicians in Washington.

When people called it politically courageous, I laughed. As someone who had been a captain in the Army and volunteered to deploy to Afghanistan as an intelligence officer, I've never understood the term "political courage," because I've served with men and women who had true courage and were making real sacrifices for the country. Deciding to run for United States Senate doesn't require courage.

I ran because I had an argument I wanted to make about the future of our country, and I thought the Senate was the best place to make that argument and push progressive policies that would lift everyone up. My strategy was pretty straightforward: As a proud progressive running for Senate in a red state, I simply said what I believed.

I learned that lesson—to simply say what I believe—early on in my political career. It was in my first race—for state representative in Kansas City. I was a twenty-six-year-old who had just recently gotten back from my tour in Afghanistan and was running against two much more well-known opponents. In fact, no one really knew me. Everybody said, "Nice young man, probably gonna come in a distant third."

But I ran for two main reasons: Originally, I was running because the Republican governor took health care away from Missourians who needed it most, and I wanted to fight back. By the time I came home from my deployment to Afghanistan—the first time in my life when I was truly negatively impacted by decisions made by politicians—my view of the world had changed. Political calculations, not military strategy, seemed to be what guided decisions in Washington about Iraq and Afghanistan. For me, state-level decisions like cutting Medicaid were no different, and I wanted to be in a position to make decisions based on what was right, not what was beneficial politically.

In that race for state representative, I knocked on 20,000 doors to make my case to voters face-to-face. I don't remember all of those doors, but I do remember a lesson I learned at one of the very first ones.

I was already pretty nervous when the voter came to his door. He asked me about an issue (I don't even remember what it was now), and I told him what I thought about it. He didn't agree with me. I was still new to this, and I didn't know any better, so I started doing what I'd seen politicians on TV shows do. I basically started acting. I tried to convince him that our views weren't really different. I was trying to make him think that my position really was the same as his, even though we both knew it wasn't.

From the look on the guy's face, it wasn't working at all. I started wondering if running for office was such a great idea. But then I kind of just blurted out, "Well, I guess we don't agree on this, but I'm just trying to do what I think is best."

As I was about to walk away dejected, he shocked me when he said, "Yeah, that's fair. OK, I'll vote for you. And you can put a sign out there if you want." I knew from then on I needed to just say what I believed and make my argument, and I hoped voters would appreciate my honesty. Hoped they would know I was running for the right reason. And then hoped they would vote for me. With that approach, I won when no one thought I could.

Every time I've run for office, it was because there was some elected position in the way of my getting something done. When I ran for state representative, it was because our governor had just cut thousands of people off from Medicaid, and I wanted to fight to undo those cuts. When I ran for secretary of state, it was because I wanted to fight back against voter suppression. And when I ran for Senate, it was because I wanted to protect Obamacare, to make sure our veterans and current members of the military were taken care of, and to pass a middle-class tax cut.

And now, I'm fighting to ensure that every eligible American has the right to cast a ballot. I started Let America Vote in February 2017, just a few months after losing my Senate race, to make sure politicians can't change the electorate to help them win reelection. I have a platform and am using it. Everyone reading this book has a platform, too, so I hope you think about how you're using yours.

Whether you win or lose, your motivation for why you ran for office in the first place will always be there with you. So my advice to everyone involved in politics is to be honest with yourself and everyone else about why you're running and what you believe. Win or lose, you always have to get up the day after the election and start again.

JENNIFER CARROLL FOY

House of Delegates // Virginia's 2nd District // Elected in 2017

I ANNOUNCED THAT I WAS running for the Virginia House of Delegates in February 2017.

Three weeks later, I found out I was pregnant—with twins.

I don't question blessings. I take things as they come—even if they come in twos. With the support of my husband and my campaign team, I kept moving forward. I knocked on doors with swollen ankles. I made phone calls while battling morning sickness. I scheduled meetings with local leaders over breakfast so that I could make my doctors' appointments in the afternoon and continue to work as a full-time public defender.

Two days before the primary election, I was put on bed rest. I worked the phones from home. My team worked to get out the vote. It was hard. My husband had to deflect volunteers and reporters who were asking where I was. I wanted to be out there, at the polls, ensuring that voters had the opportunity to look me in the face and see how important this election was, and what was at stake, just one more time before they cast their votes.

But I stayed put. Because even though the election was big, the lives I carried were so much bigger.

It was close, but I won the primary. Not long after that, I went into labor. My beautiful twin sons, Alex and Xander, were born prematurely. They were small and in critical condition. My husband and I spent hours alongside our boys in the neonatal ICU. I spent a while recovering in the hospital myself. Still, we kept the campaign moving forward.

The hospital became our headquarters. My field director, Josh Crandell, met me in my hospital room, where we discussed messaging and strategies for the general election. We conducted interviews by phone for a campaign team. In between donor calls, my nurses would help me into and out of bed because I couldn't walk.

Through it all, people told me that I couldn't do it. They said that I couldn't be a mother, an attorney, a wife, and a candidate. But I put my head down and ignored the naysayers and got to work. I used their words as fuel for my fire. It wasn't the first time I'd had to do that.

I grew up not far from the Virginia Military Institute (VMI). At the time, it was one of the top military colleges in the country. Only it didn't accept women.

In 1996, a case challenging the school's all-male policy made its way to the Supreme Court. It was a hot topic at my high school. My male classmates argued that women didn't have the stamina or the strength, mental or physical, to graduate from one of the most challenging colleges in the country. Of course, I thought differently.

So, when Justice Ruth Bader Ginsburg announced the Supreme Court's decision that VMI had to accept women, I read her opinion with intense interest. She wrote about how the history of the Constitution is one of increasing inclusion. She said, "There is no reason to believe that the admission of women capable of all the activities required of VMI cadets would destroy the Institute rather than enhance its capacity to serve the 'more perfect union.'"

In that moment, I decided I had to go to VMI. I enrolled as one of the first women of color to attend, and later graduate from, the college. On my first day, they shaved my head and said, "Welcome to VMI."

Much like politics, VMI didn't change any of its standards because I was a woman. No concessions were made. I ran the same twenty miles uphill with fifty pounds on my back. I crawled through the same mud.

I PUT MY
★ ★
HEAD DOWN
AND
IGNORED THE
NAYSAYERS
AND
GOT TO WORK

My best guy friend bet me a dollar that I wouldn't last a year. Well, I won that bet.

When I was young, my grandmother told me that if I didn't like something, then I should do something about it. I listened. That's how I ended up graduating from VMI, that's how I ended up becoming a public defender, and that's how I ended up running for office.

Like so many people, I woke up on November 9, 2016, in disbelief. I went to sleep early the night before, trusting that the American people would never elect someone as intolerant or incompetent as the Republican candidate for president.

When I found out that he'd won, I felt helpless. A reality-television star was going to be president instead of one of the most qualified, experienced public servants ever to run for the office.

I couldn't believe that our country had given in to fear and bigotry. I couldn't understand how Donald Trump's racist and sexist antics were not disqualifying. I was so angry that he was not being held accountable for his attacks on veterans, people with disabilities, immigrants, and women.

Still, it wasn't as if Trump had just happened. For years, I'd watched the General Assembly in Virginia. Led by Republicans, it perpetuated attack after attack on women, people living in poverty, and immigrants. Its members failed to expand Medicaid or improve our infrastructure. Virginia had become notorious for our school-to-prison pipeline. They did nothing to address it.

I didn't like it, so I had to do something about it. I had to run for public office.

I knew it wasn't going to be easy. I was a woman of color, a first-time candidate, and a progressive running for a seat long held by Republicans. The odds were not in my favor.

But I knew my purpose. I was fighting for a fairer, stronger, and more just Virginia. I believed that message was important. So important that I was willing to walk up to a neighbor proudly wearing a shirt with a Confederate flag on it. It read, "Don't tread on me." We were at a fair, and I introduced myself. I asked him and his wife for their votes. They were shocked, and it turned out that they didn't live in my district. But I was glad I said hello.

After all, there has to be more that connects us than separates us. There just has to be.

No matter what, I kept moving forward. I was determined to win. I put my head down and when things got tough or people started to count me out, I remembered the words of my grandmother: "I can show you better than I can tell you."

I did that, and I won.

PRAMILA JAYAPAL

U.S. House of Representatives //
Washington's 7ᵗʰ Congressional District // Elected in 2016

I NEVER THOUGHT I WOULD run for office. I always considered myself an outside organizer, an activist helping to build the movement for justice. In fact, even being an organizer was a far cry from what my parents wanted for me so many decades ago when they sent me to this country from India, by myself, at the age of sixteen.

When my parents used the last $5,000 in their bank account to send me across the ocean to go to college, they had determined that I would have the most economic security if I pursued becoming a doctor, lawyer, or businessperson. We had very little money back then and no Skype, so I was allowed only one phone call home a year. I still remember using that phone call my sophomore year of college to tell my father that instead of majoring in economics, I planned to major in English literature. I had to hold the phone away from my ear as he yelled that he didn't send me here to learn how to speak English—I already knew how to speak English! I promised him that I would get the same job with an English degree that I would have with an economics degree, and I went on to work on Wall Street for an investment bank and then to get a master's in business administration.

I've always believed that doing things that help you understand what you don't want to do is as important as doing the things that help you understand what you love doing. Those early experiences in business helped me build management, organizational, and financial skills that would be important later on as I started an immigrant-rights organization and entered the political world. After that, I spent ten years working in global health and development, on health projects around the world, and then living for two years in villages in India.

Then 9/11 happened. It changed the course of my life.

Newly divorced and with a young toddler, I woke up to the news of the hijackers flying planes into the World Trade Center. I knew right away that things were about to change—for our country as a whole, but especially for brown people like me; for Muslims, Sikhs, and immigrants of all kinds who would be even more unjustly profiled in the wake of these attacks. Within days, we were seeing hate crimes against Arabs, Muslims, and South Asians. Women in hijab were being attacked. Kids in schools were being bullied. Turbaned cab drivers were being physically assaulted. I knew I had to do something.

So I started what would end up being the largest immigrant-advocacy organization in Washington state. Originally called Hate Free Zone, later OneAmerica, the organization created strong multiethnic, multisectoral coalitions to address not only hate crimes but also incursions on civil rights by our own government. We successfully sued the Bush administration to stop the deportation of thousands of Somalis across the country, took on secret detentions of Arab Americans and Muslims, organized around comprehensive immigration reform, and led the largest voter registration drive in the history of Washington state, registering more than 23,000 new American citizens to vote. After twelve incredible years at the helm of the organization, I stepped aside to spend some time with my son—who was close to high school graduation—and to reflect on what I wanted to do next.

Throughout my time at OneAmerica, many of our community members and leaders suggested that I run for office. I always demurred. Sure, we knew that we had to engage in politics—not just policy. We not only registered voters, we turned people out to vote, and we started a separate organization called OneAmerica Votes to build political power and endorse immigrant candidates for office. But running for office myself wasn't appealing then—I saw myself as that outside organizer, not the insider politician.

Then, in 2014, the state senator representing my district announced he would retire. Several candidates were already in the race, and I began receiving calls to run. At first, I offered the same answer I had always given: "No, thanks, it's not for me."

But then I realized something. I realized that I was tired of trying to get other people to do the things I, and our communities, felt should be done. I also wanted to see more people like me in office—women, people of color, immigrants. And I realized that we organizers were ceding important political space by not thinking about elected office as another platform for organizing.

I decided to run for that state senate seat. I won, becoming the first South Asian ever elected to the state legislature and the only woman of color in the state senate!

When the congressman who represented the Seattle area decided to retire after twenty-eight years, again there were numerous people in the race already. Still, my phone started ringing off the hook from national activists and leaders around the country who wanted me to run. At the same time, some of the political insiders who heard I was thinking about running tried to talk me out of it. "There are others who are more seasoned and can raise the money needed for this level of race," I was told. "Maybe you should stay in the senate longer and run later?"

That kind of talk only made me more determined to run—and to win. As a minority woman of color, I've had to work hard for everything I have, and I'm not afraid of that. As one of the union leaders here has said about me, "She doesn't have a give-up bone in her body!"

I ran the campaign the way I wanted to run it. I hired a smart, talented campaign director who believed in field strategy and had run field for the Obama campaign in Ohio. We divided the district into six parts, each with a designated organizer. I hired my longtime organizing director from OneAmerica as my field director—a brilliant movement builder from El Salvador who could pull together and inspire our six organizers and our 1,200 volunteers who believed in the future-focused vision of our campaign. Together, we knocked on more than 120,000 doors and made more than 270,000 phone calls to voters. I engaged young people and folks of color who are traditionally left out of politics. We talked to all voters, not just the "likely" ones who had voted before.

This field component was a huge and important part of my campaign. I love knocking on doors. In my book, it is a privilege to have someone open the door to a total stranger and tell her their hopes, dreams, and fears. The stories I heard grounded me and our team in what we were fighting for and gave texture to policy. We heard about people who were one health-care crisis away from bankruptcy; about families ripped apart by opioids; about rents going up, leaving people near eviction. We heard, too, about surviving breast cancer, about babies and grandbabies just born, and we were invited in many a time for coffee or a meal. I got to really know my district—physically and emotionally. Opening the door to a stranger knocking is the ultimate act of generosity.

I knew that I could only do this my way, by putting my own story and values into the campaign. I talked about my immigrant experience and made it part of who I was and what I would bring as a congress member, even though consultants sometimes advised against raising any background that makes you seem "different." But it was precisely my story that made me want to fight for the things I believed in. Even though the majority of the voters in the district were white, I thought they would appreciate where I came from and the values of hard work, resilience, and courage that were ingrained in me because of my experiences.

I also refused to take corporate PAC money. That meant that I had to raise all my funds through individuals and noncorporate PACs such as women's groups and unions. In the end, I raised almost $3 million through 82,000 individuals across the country who contributed an average of $23 apiece. I was running on issues such as ending Citizens United, but I told everyone we didn't need to wait for that reform; we could actually reform the way we run and finance our campaigns right now.

Even though some consultants say that it is not worth it to spend ' money on yard signs, I have always seen the matter differently. If someone takes a yard sign early in the campaign and puts it in their yard, they have to walk by it every single day and think about why they have it there.

Neighbors will ask about the candidate and why they are supporting the campaign. A yard sign means something—it means that the person who has it trusts the candidate and will stand up for him or her. That is gold in a campaign—entire streets can be won because of that yard sign. Our signs were an unusual pink and purple, and to this day I have constituents come up and tell me that they loved the sign, and some even still have it in their yards!

We used television, social media, and mail to amplify the story, because we had to reach 750,000 people. I had the backing of every labor union, women's organization, and many environmental leaders. But my opponents were formidable and they had raised an almost equivalent amount of money and had an independent lobby come in to spend more money on attacking me. I just had to stay focused on what I was trying to achieve and keep my eyes on the road ahead.

Everything we did—down to our pink-and-purple yard signs—was different, but it had to be. My tagline was "Bold. Progressive. Unafraid," and my team was the same way. I wanted to call people in to a strong, bold, progressive vision. I wanted people to feel what I felt: that we could do this together, create a different future for too many who have been left behind or go to bed worried about how they will make it the next day. The stakes were high. If I won, I'd be the first woman to ever represent Washington's Seventh Congressional District, and I'd be the first Indian American woman ever to hold a seat in the U.S. House of Representatives.

Today, I'm so proud to represent this district in Congress and to be one of only about 11,000 people in the history of this country who have served in Congress—and one of even fewer people of color or women. I love this job—it's hard, demanding, and requires real sacrifices not only from members of Congress but from our families. But I wake up every day and know what I am fighting for, and I bring everything I have to that struggle. And although my path was far from linear—I never did become a doctor, lawyer, or businessperson—I believe that everything I have ever done in my life helped prepare me for this moment, a critical time in our country's history when we are fighting for our soul and our future.

I recently bought a T-shirt with a quote from J. R. R. Tolkien that summed it all up perfectly: "Not all those who wander are lost." The roads

WE ARE FIGHTING FOR OUR SOUL AND OUR FUTURE

I have followed often involved leaps of faith, but I trusted my instincts and I believed I could do anything. Every experience helped me understand more about who I was and what I wanted to spend my life doing. When I felt that I needed to make a change, I followed my gut. When things were uncertain, I believed in myself. When I wanted something done, I fought for it.

My message, especially to women and people of color out there, is this: refuse to be intimidated, minimized, or patronized. Bring love and generosity into everything you do. Think about what you want to do, not what you want to be. Don't be afraid to wander—and trust that you won't get lost. Those roads will all lead to the right place.

ALEXANDRA CHANDLER

U.S. House of Representatives //
Massachusetts's 3ʳᵈ Congressional District // Candidate in 2018

ON SEPTEMBER 11, 1994, I tried to stop my father from dying. It was a nice Sunday afternoon. He was in no position to drive a car that day, between his severe multiple sclerosis, the prescription drugs I knew he was abusing, and perhaps alcohol. But, despite my protests, he did drive. And he never came back home.

Five days later I found myself standing in front of a few dozen friends and family, some very nice flowers, and my father's coffin. It was a beautiful Friday morning. I was holding a few pages of handwritten notes—the eulogy I had written for my father on behalf of myself and my younger brother.

In that eulogy, I spoke of gratitude in the face of sadness. I spoke of how our father had taught me and my brother to love literature and science, about how he gave us his painfully dry sense of humor. I conjured up images. My dad reading Tolkien to me, then encouraging me to read the pages myself. The two of us shivering outside with a telescope, looking for Halley's Comet. And then I exposed the raw pain I was feeling, my sadness and the unrecoverable hurt that I would never see him again in this world, but that I hoped to in the next world I want to believe is there.

When I walked down from the pulpit, I was so overcome with emotion that I slipped on a step and nearly fell right onto my father's coffin, steadying myself on a railing just in time.

The rest is a blur. The cemetery. His grave, a grave I've visited many times over the years.

I didn't realize it, but at the reception my family and our friends were talking about the eulogy I'd given. I was a quiet kid. I actually hated the sound of my own voice. So people weren't expecting that I could connect with them the way I had. Months later, my mom told me that there was talk—amid all the sadness—that I could have a future in politics.

But there was a reason I hated my voice. There was a reason that I didn't use it much to connect. My voice didn't fit who I was. My whole body didn't. What my friends and family didn't know then was that I am transgender.

They didn't know that I had realized I was transgender a few years earlier. They didn't know that, in the days leading up to my father's funeral, I threw out all of my carefully hidden stashes of women's clothing. They didn't know, and I had decided I could never tell them. My family had suffered through my father's addiction, his progressive disability, his problems with unemployment, and my parents' divorce. I couldn't add to their burden. So I suffered with mine alone.

I threw myself into academics for my final year of high school and then university—first at the University of Pennsylvania, then at Brown University. I had a few friends but kept them at a distance. I resumed a habit I had back in middle school of carrying a pocket novel with me to ensure I could always retreat from conversation. I had little to say—and I didn't want to say much.

After my father died, I started dating Cathy. I told her on our third date that I felt better when cross-dressed or gender ambiguous but felt I couldn't give in to it because I was afraid of wanting to transition, and I couldn't do that to my family. She wasn't scared away. She said she actually thought it was admirable that I was so in touch with my sense of self and that I should just take it one day at a time, as she would.

Cathy and I have been together for twenty-three years, and ten years ago we got married. But on September 11, 2001, seven years after my dad died, I almost lost her.

After I heard the news of the attack on the World Trade Center, I spent hours in our Brooklyn studio apartment pacing and crying and screaming. I knew Cathy was on a subway train somewhere in Lower Manhattan, coming home after an early-morning errand. I imagined the horror of her forever lost in a crumbled subway tunnel. I imagined it with the mind of someone for whom September 11 already meant death.

I begged and pleaded with God. I didn't hear any answer. I bargained and offered up my own life, dedicating myself to service, to kindness, to focus on others over myself. Just let Cathy come home. I don't know if it was an answer, but I did receive a call from a pay phone two hours later. It was Cathy, who had walked out of Brooklyn Bridge–City Hall station. She walked home across the Manhattan Bridge, covered in the dust of the unspeakable.

I kept up my end of the bargain. As a third-year law student, I decided to apply to intelligence community agencies rather than corporate law firms. I had studied the Central Asian states and spoke Russian, and I felt I had something to offer. I could help protect our country and prevent others from spending hours in a hellish purgatory or living a nightmare of loss that never ended.

By the time I finally got through a security clearance process and received my offer letter from the Office of Naval Intelligence (ONI) in 2004, something else had changed. In the time since 9/11, I had focused my vow to be kinder inward as well as outward. I experimented more and more with my gender expression after years of containment. I was increasingly androgynous in appearance—some friends barely ever saw me in what we increasingly called "boy mode." Some never even knew my male name.

And yet, I feared gender transition. I bargained with myself, rationing different amounts of time presenting as male, female, or someone in between. I wanted to live my truth but didn't know if I could. And I hoped that the fulfillment of a career in service to my country might banish the need to force this truth back into the shadows.

Walking in the door in May 2004, I was far from the typical ONI civilian intelligence analyst—at that time, many were former sailors and soldiers. True to form since I was a kid, I kept people at a distance, not letting them see or know my authentic self. And yet I was accepted, made friends, and fell in love with my mission area: analysis to counter the spread of weapons of mass destruction from countries like North Korea and to prevent the transfer of weapons to conflict zones and terrorist groups.

By June 2005, I couldn't un-see the truth any longer, and I decided to start my gender transition. However, with no policies to protect my rights at the time, no precedent of a successful transition at ONI, I assumed I would need to leave. When I came out to my supervisor, it was mostly to give more than the usual amount of notice to ensure that someone else would be ready to take over the critical elements of my job.

Instead of firing me or nudging me toward the door, my supervisor championed the plan for my gender transition at work. The civilian and military chain of command did not waver in their collective desire to learn and to do the right thing, even at tough moments. I learned as I never had before what leadership looked like. In June 2006, I started my life presenting as Alexandra full-time.

Having learned those lessons of leadership so directly, I then unexpectedly became a leader myself. For the first time in my life, I was not hiding my authentic self: I was bringing all of me to work. And in doing so, I found I had a knack for unlocking the talent of others—through storytelling, through my own vulnerability, through connecting with people's deeper aspirations. I finally saw what my family and friends had seen in me under the shadow of death in 1994.

But now, I no longer hated my voice. I owned it and used it.

I was promoted again and again and again. Soon, I had an official photo on the agency's "leadership wall." For five years I served as a division chief, directing the activities of teams of analysts targeting the spread of WMDs and weapons worldwide. I loved my job, my colleagues, and my life.

I might still be doing that job but for the fact that my wife and I then had two children. My sons, William and George, and the 2016 election set me on a different path.

DID I
ANSWER
★ THE CALL ★
TO SERVE
WHEN IT CAME?

Having two small children and an active career in the intelligence community was not easy. My hours were unpredictable and came with stresses, from domestic crises like government shutdowns to actual foreign crises. My wife and I increasingly felt the absence of our families, still living back in New England.

The 2016 presidential election pulled our hearts farther northward. The shock of the result was a reminder of how unpredictable and short life could be. I was about to turn forty, approaching the age my father was when he died.

Cathy and I decided to move to Massachusetts in the spring of 2017. We gave our notice to our employers of thirteen years. I saw something comparatively quiet in my future—perhaps work as a nonprofit executive, in management consulting, or with a socially responsible corporation. We sold our house and began our move north in the summer.

However, something else was happening in tandem with our plans. Just days after the election, friends were sending me messages through the She Should Run website, telling me that I should run for office. I had always been intellectually interested in politics but had told friends that politics either had to get much worse or much better before I would consider it. Still, thinking about the longer-term future, I signed up for candidate and campaign trainings over the spring and summer. I thought that maybe I would run for school board someday.

Then our home district member of Congress, Niki Tsongas, unexpectedly announced in August of 2017 that she would not run for reelection. Friends—both old and new—started e-mailing me and calling me that day, urging me to run for her seat.

"You are a Russian-speaking lawyer and worked for thirteen years in the intelligence community."

"You know North Korea and Iran."

"You have experience with community health care and are a middle-class mom."

"You bring your experience with your father's addiction and death to the opioid epidemic."

"You have learned how to work across divisions against the world's toughest problems. We need that in Congress. Run!"

These reasons eventually persuaded me that I could be a good member of Congress. But the reason I decided to run was something an old friend asked me. He asked me if I knew I was the most qualified to be our district's next congresswoman, and if at this moment in our history I choose not to do it, what would I see in years to come when I looked into William's and George's eyes? What did I do to help? Did I answer the call to serve when it came?

I answered the call. I decided to run.

SHOSHANNA KELLY

Board of Aldermen // Nashua, New Hampshire // Elected in 2017

I DON'T WATCH MUCH TV. But on November 8, 2016, I was glued to mine. That morning I put on the closest thing I had to a pantsuit—a jacket over a "Nasty Woman" T-shirt. I went to my polling location, and I proudly brought my six-year-old daughter into the voting booth with me.

Less than twelve hours later, I was on my couch, hoping for a miracle. As the winds began to change, and the states turned to red, my hope turned into despair. I called my best friend. We cried together. I went to bed with tears rolling down my face, hoping to wake up and find out that this was just a horrible nightmare.

I opened my eyes the next morning and dragged myself from my bed, last night's tears still on my cheeks. It wasn't a nightmare. How could I face the world? How could we get through what was coming next?

For me, it wasn't about the man. It was about what he stood for. I just couldn't fathom how it was 2016 and my biracial daughter would grow up with a president who was endorsed by the KKK. It was beyond my capacity to understand that there were millions of American people who could look at such a reprehensible human being and elect him as our leader.

My daughter saved me that day. She crawled into my bed and took my face in her hands. She asked, "Is Trump going to crazy our country?"

Something stirred inside me as I promised, "The adults are taking care of it, baby."

It was both an innocent question and a call to action. My daughter asked me to show up. She asked me to fight. And there was no choice but to do exactly that.

As November turned to December and December turned to January, the despair started to turn back to hope. Across the country, people were ready to make a statement and demand change. That feeling permeated every corner of New Hampshire as we trudged over the snow and ice for the Women's March.

My daughter held her sign and yelled with excitement as we wound through Nashua's cobblestone streets. As we approached the hill in the Common, we saw thousands of men, women, and children with rallying cries on their posters and their faces.

The crowd took my breath away. In that moment, I knew that the 200,000 people gathered below would help me make good on my promise to my daughter. Together, we were going to fix things.

I separated from our group for a moment and took it all in. Tears streamed down my cold, flushed cheeks: It was time to get to work.

A few weeks later, a simple—but huge—thing happened. A good friend sat me down for coffee and asked me if I had ever considered running for office. To be perfectly honest, I hadn't. But suddenly it clicked. If I wanted to create change, this was one way I could.

Now, I will be the first to fully admit that when I decided to run for office, I had no idea how to run a campaign. I didn't know what being an alderman-at-large in Nashua meant or that the aldermen governed our city. I didn't own a blazer or have a single pair of practical heels. But I knew things couldn't stay the same. So I had to run.

I started asking questions and people started showing up for me. Whether they were helping with logistics or providing moral support, I quickly had a group behind me. My friends knocked doors in the rain, taught me how to raise money, spent late nights making signs, and lifted me up on those days when I just wanted to give up. And there were many.

Campaigning was one of the toughest things I have ever done. But it was also really rewarding. I found myself waking up on Saturday mornings eager to spend hours at my neighbors' doors, just talking about our city. I started calling friends and family, telling them my dream, and asking them to help me achieve it. I began figuring out what I stood for, making speeches, and putting together events. Every time it was a little easier. Every time I was a little stronger.

I often felt underqualified and scared. The voice in my head would say, "Who do you think you are?" But every time I looked at my little girl and remembered my promise, I swallowed all of that.

She was so proud of me. That alone was enough to make me feel like a winner. She knocked doors and held signs. She came to every speech. As days turned into months and the summer turned to fall, she kept me going. She was watching me, and I wasn't going to let her down.

On Election Day in 2017, I woke up at five in the morning and donned my pink "Vote for Sho" T-shirt. My breath became steam as I crawled into my bitterly cold car packed with campaign materials. Over the next fourteen hours, I went to all nine of our ward voting locations, shaking hands, smiling, and drinking lots of coffee. Everyone in my crew was nervous. We all had no idea what to expect. But I knew we had done everything we could.

At eight in the evening, the polls closed. I felt like collapsing on the spot. I just wanted to hide. I turned off my phone, drove home in silence, and climbed into a hot shower. I stood there for a long time—in fact, I think my husband finally knocked on the door and told me it was time for the Election Night party.

I fumbled with my dress and shoes as I ran every scenario through my head. I told myself that, no matter what, I was not going to cry. When my phone finally rang, it felt far away. My friend's voice came through. "It's early, but I'd like to be the first to say congratulations, Alderwoman Kelly."

A wave of joy, disbelief, and excitement washed over me. I was the underdog, the unknown candidate. I'd run against a former mayoral candidate, two incumbents, a lawyer, and an investor—all white men. But I won.

Still dazed, I walked into the party. There was loud applause. Then the big news was announced from the stage—we had just made history! In

I WAS NOW
THE
LEADER
I HAD BEEN
HOPING FOR

Nashua, we elected seven women to our board of fifteen. We voted in the first two women of color and three people under age forty.

In the weeks following the election, I would sit in my car, listening to a song or talk radio, and a wave of pure exhilaration would come over me. Pounding the steering wheel with tears in my eyes, I would try to wrap my head around what we had achieved together.

I was now the leader I had been hoping for.

My yearlong journey ended how it had begun. On a cold New England morning, I packed up my husband and daughter and headed to the second Women's March at our capitol. As we walked up to the rally, I grinned widely at the sea of pink hats and protest signs.

At the first march, I remember thinking that rallying was nice, but we needed to act. But looking back, I realized that the march was action. It was action that moved tens of thousands to run for office in 2017. It was action that moved even more to volunteer and vote.

This time, I wasn't just marching; I was speaking. As I paced next to the podium, I tried to shake off the feeling that I didn't belong on that stage. Then there was no time left to doubt it; my name was called, and I climbed the stairs. I took a deep breath and looked at my daughter. It was time to share my story and invite more women in.

The next few minutes were a blur. But I remember I got my message out: run for office. We can't keep trying to lobby the other side and hope to succeed. Instead, we must put smart, hardworking people into office who will listen and act on behalf of every person of every race and background in this country.

I told that crowd that if I'd learned nothing else in the last year, it was that anyone can run for office. You do not need to have an MBA or a law degree. You do not need to look like the usual suspects—and you certainly don't have to act like them. You just need to step up, speak up, and work hard.

That's what I try to do every day. Because I know my daughter is watching, and I will never forget my promise to her.

KATE BROWN

Governor // Oregon // Elected in 2016

★

I GREW UP IN A stable middle-class neighborhood in Minnesota.

My parents worked hard. My father was an ophthalmologist; my mother supported the family at home. And I knew from an early age that education was the key to a better life. My parents raised me and my siblings to believe that if we worked hard and played by the rules, we could do anything we wanted to. For me, that meant going to law school.

As a lawyer I believed I would have the tools to help create justice in this world.

I'd grown up in suburbia and, like so many kids my age from the Midwest, I looked to the western horizon to see the future. Since I couldn't see past the mountains of Colorado, I went to college in Boulder to get ready for law school and do more than my share of skiing.

It was the late seventies and America was coming out of two decades that started with Rachel Carson's 1962 *Silent Spring* and ended with the oil crisis of 1979. In just a few short years, environmentalism went from a movement on college campuses to a reality at the gas pump.

If there was anywhere to be to change the world, I thought, it was in environmental law. So, when I graduated from the University of Colorado at Boulder, I again went west, to Oregon. I landed at the renowned environmental law program at Lewis & Clark College in Portland. There was nothing in the country like it. We were learning how to put the kinship we had developed with the natural world into practice in the courtroom.

But after three years of study, I realized that the chances for an environmental lawyer to make major changes in the world were slim at that time. Most graduates were heading off to defend corporations instead of our ecosystems. I couldn't see myself in a boardroom, cleaning up a company's mess and figuring out how not to pay for it. Disengaged, I continued pushing through law school while searching for a career path that felt genuine to me.

At the time Portland was, as it is today, a progressive town, where the women's movement that was born in the late sixties could still be found in bookstores, coffee shops, and even bars.

I volunteered at a women's health clinic and truly found my place in the community. I made friends and we built a support network. And I learned that in helping a single person navigate the barriers that all women face in health care, we were making it easier for the next woman, and for the woman after that, and, eventually, for all of us.

With every patient, we were discovering ways to work around each new obstacle that men had put in the way of women's rights to make decisions about their own bodies. We were also proving that changing the world doesn't necessarily happen all at once; it happens one person at a time. And it felt revolutionary.

That's a long way of saying I learned that the real reason I wanted to be a lawyer was to help people.

So, after graduation, I got a job at the Portland Feminist Women's Health Center. Degree in hand, whole life in front of me, I walked in the door, ready to put passion into practice in the real world. I was filled with anticipation for my first assignment. My new boss walked up to me and gave me the warmest smile. I felt I had made the right decision and could see the path for my life clearly set out in front of me.

Then she told me I was laid off. To say the least, the first day of my new life didn't turn out quite as I'd expected.

Still, I was fortunate to have a law degree, and I went to work at a law firm as an attorney representing families. It wasn't what I thought I would do when I walked across the stage at graduation, but I was still helping people and, in an incremental way, helping change the world.

As it turned out, many of the most important lessons I learned early in my law career came not only when I was helping others navigate challenges but when I was navigating my own.

As an attorney, I learned firsthand what it's like to be paid less—substantially less—than the male attorney in the office next to me. I also learned firsthand what it's like to be afraid of losing my job because, at the time, I was in a relationship with a woman. It was hard to put a part of who I was aside when I left our home each morning and to walk into that law firm and pretend that I was someone else.

I vowed that if I ever had the opportunity, I would do everything I could to make sure no one else had to face that kind of discrimination or live in fear.

A few years later I got my opportunity. I became an advocate for a women's rights organization in Oregon. I lobbied the legislature on policies to improve the health and wellness of Oregon women. This included improving domestic-violence laws, stepping up child-support enforcement, and ensuring that Oregon became one of the first states in the country to pass family medical leave. When the bill was signed, I stood with other advocates to mark the moment right behind Barbara Roberts, the first woman governor of Oregon.

Standing with Governor Roberts and several women who had advocated so hard on behalf of those who couldn't speak for themselves, I realized that I could make a difference. I could work to make Oregon a better place for all of our families. And piece by piece, law by law, person by person, I could help change the world.

That's when I got a phone call I will never forget. My state senator at the time, Shirley Gold, said that my state representative was giving up her seat, and asked if I wanted to seek the appointment.

I was young. I didn't have a job. And I didn't have a family at the time. I said, "Hell, yes."

In just a few short weeks, I was a newly minted member of the Oregon legislature and getting ready for the next legislative session. I knew immediately I wanted to keep the seat. We were passing laws, breaking down barriers, and having a great time. I didn't want to stop!

But the person I had been appointed to replace didn't get the state government job she was seeking, and I got another phone call. She told me that she wanted her seat back. But I wanted to keep the seat. Then it sank in. I'd have to fight for my seat in the primary. And the race wasn't going to be easy.

Well, I was doomed—everyone said so. She was well known; I was not. That made it all but impossible to raise money for my campaign. But I had two things going for me: guts and determination. If I couldn't out-fund-raise my opponent, I would outwork her.

I figured I had nothing to lose, and I became the human embodiment of what it means to run for office. I knocked on hundreds of doors. My family and friends spent all their free time volunteering on the streets of Southeast Portland. We left no stone unturned and no door without a piece of campaign literature.

And in the end, I won—by seven votes. Seven. Votes. Even twenty-five years later, people still come up to me and say that they were my seventh vote. Everyone who voted for me believes that he or she was the reason I won. And you know what? They absolutely were.

Any time you wonder if you should bother voting, or if your vote even counts, you should think of me. Your voice matters, and your vote is your voice.

I went on to serve for seventeen years as a state legislator in the Oregon House of Representatives and State Senate. But, most important, I worked to ensure that those whose voices had been drowned out for so long were being heard in our capitol.

Among many other historic laws, I passed legislation to require insurance companies to cover contraceptives, to prohibit discrimination based on sexual orientation and gender identity, and to legalize same-sex relationships through civil unions.

And while I was Senate majority leader, in 2006, we turned Oregon blue. For the first time in fifteen years, Democrats were in control of both chambers of the legislature and the governor's office. Oregonians knew that the policies we put into place were in the best interests of our state.

In 2008, I was elected secretary of state and, among many of my job duties, I was working to ensure that all eligible Oregonians were able to have their voices heard in the election process. Early on we passed a law to create Oregon's first online voter registration system. Later, I developed a bill to create the country's first automatic voter registration program.

But in 2015, I got another call I never expected. The current governor was resigning and, as secretary of state, I was next in line to lead the state. In just five days, I would become the second woman to ever be governor of Oregon.

On the day I was sworn in as Oregon's thirty-eighth governor, the reasons I became a lawmaker in the first place, twenty-five years earlier, were again front and center. I experienced what it's like to be labeled—to have my first two decades of public service eclipsed by a single phrase, "the nation's first openly bisexual governor," which appeared after my name in virtually every headline worldwide.

But, like every other obstacle that had been put in a woman's way over the years, I found a way to get past it. And the first bill I signed created our historic automatic voter registration system. In just three years as governor I worked successfully to raise the state's minimum wage, ensure a fair work schedule, and guarantee paid sick leave. We made record investments in education and signed a law giving every Oregonian access to a professionally invested retirement account. I made Oregon the first state in the country to take action to end the use of coal power, putting Oregon at the forefront of the clean energy movement. And every session since I've become governor, we have passed commonsense gun-safety legislation to keep our children and families safe.

None of this would have happened if it wasn't for those who voted for me way back in 1992 and all those who helped me along the way.

As governor, I am doing what I've always wanted to do. Helping change Oregon for the better, one person at a time.

And you know what? It still feels revolutionary.

MICHELLE DE LA ISLA

Mayor // Topeka, Kansas // Elected in 2017

MY DAD WASN'T AROUND. My mom drank. And my grandparents helped raise me. Some of my family members felt like I wouldn't amount to much, and they weren't afraid to tell me so. I felt insignificant. But I wanted to be heard.

I would hide in my closet to read books and write poetry and dream of a better life. And I would be asked, "Why do you love reading those books? Do you think you're better than us?"

So I left. I was nearly eighteen. I went out for a jog and just never came back. It wasn't easy. Especially at first. I didn't have a permanent home, so I surfed couches. I went to college and failed my classes and had to withdraw. I got involved with the wrong guy. And then I got pregnant. I called my mom to tell her, and again she told me that I would never amount to anything.

I was determined to prove her wrong.

I went back to my college and begged to be let back in, and, thanks to an interim director who believed in second chances, they said OK. I tried to be the best mom I could for my son, Erick. I started singing in church, too. My priest saw how well I was doing and encouraged me to move from Puerto Rico to the mainland to continue my education.

I developed Paget's disease of the breast, which was considered breast cancer back then. My grandfather died of cancer that year, too. Undeterred, I applied to Wichita State University in Kansas. With the support of a vocational rehabilitation program and a lot of student loans, I was on my way.

I got my degree. I got two jobs on campus—one working for Upward Bound, a program that helps low-income students get ready for college. I taught my students biology and Spanish, and in teaching them and getting to know them, I heard echoes of my own story. I never considered myself to be anything special, but I was hell-bent on making sure that these kids knew they were special and that they could overcome their hardships and succeed. To me, that was doing good. That was leading.

I got married. I gave birth to my daughter Cristina. Then I had three jobs, one teaching biology at a community college, another running my own cleaning business, and another being office manager at the university's office of international programs.

I juggled being a wife, parenting, and working. Then I had my youngest daughter, Loraine. We moved from Wichita to Topeka. And it was there that my activism and advocacy began.

I found a job at a local nonprofit and got involved with MANA de Topeka, a group that supports Latinas in the business community. As I became more and more engaged in this work, I became more and more empowered in my life. With the support of the YWCA, I got out of my abusive marriage. I learned that I had a voice. I learned that my scars weren't shameful, but helpful. Those scars allow me to connect with others going through the same stuff and support them.

Right as everything was starting to turn around for me, a group of volunteers asked me to bring the "youth perspective" to the process of redeveloping downtown Topeka. I was humbled to be asked, and a little surprised, but I have always been up for the opportunity to learn something new. I sat in those meetings, listening to discussions on "walkability" and "urban planning," and had no clue what they were talking about, but I did know what young people were talking about, so I brought that perspective to the table.

Then came my first city council meeting. We were there to ask for funding for the redevelopment. We provided our testimony, but we were turned down. So we went back again. This time, we brought a local high school student who happened to be my mentee. Having her there made a big difference. She told the council members in no uncertain terms that she and her friends would not stay in town unless it was revitalized. That night, the vote passed.

Sparks. I can't explain it any other way. I felt sparks. There was a place that you could go and be heard, no matter how old you were or how many mistakes you'd made or how rough your life had been. There was a place where you could really make a difference. And in that moment, I knew I wanted to help lead in that place.

When my neighbor, friend, downtown revitalization partner, and city council member Larry Wolgast decided to run for mayor, people started asking if I would run for his seat. My daughters had sat through their fair share of council meetings at that point. My youngest told me, "Mom, if you run for this seat and win, you are showing us that we can do anything." That sealed the deal.

I ran and won and served on the city council for nearly five years. Sometimes that work was rewarding; sometimes it was frustrating. I'll be honest: By the end, I was almost ready to throw in the towel. Then Mayor Wolgast decided not to run for reelection in 2017. A bunch of people reached out asking if I would run, offering to support me however they could. My daughters urged me to go for it, so I did.

The race was ridiculously hard. I was the first to announce. There were rumblings that another council member was interested in running, and before long there were four other candidates. All white. All men.

I was the only single parent. I was also the only candidate who made it clear that I would continue working full-time while serving as mayor. People started harping on that. "How can you work and raise your kids and serve the city?" they'd ask. Working moms everywhere understand these questions all too well.

The race was supposed to be nonpartisan. However, the weekend before the primary, a postcard showed up in a few people's mailboxes. It said that I was a Democrat and one of my opponents was a Republican. That postcard made the race partisan.

Things got even worse. I'm a cancer and stroke survivor. One of my children struggles with mental health issues, so I have medical bills. After my divorce, my credit report was a mess, and I lost my home. In backrooms and boardrooms, these were the things that were being shared with donors and supporters.

But, as First Lady Michelle Obama said, "When they go low, we go high." My team of forty incredible volunteers stayed focused on knocking on doors and making calls and tweeting and posting to Facebook and placing advertisements on TV and raising money and writing personalized thank-you notes and going to Every. Single. Forum. There were more than twenty total. Basically, take what you think running a campaign like this requires and double it. We worked hard. Harder than hard.

On Saturdays, I shared a meal with my campaign team. It was my way of saying thank you. I was so grateful to my campaign managers, Nicole and Mikki, and the whole team. They devoted their free time to supporting my candidacy. What an incredible gift! And on Sundays, we rested. I went to church, cooked dinner, and spent time with my girls. I caught up on my sleep, too.

Even though we outworked, out-fund-raised, and out-marketed our opponent, the race was close. Too close.

November 7, 2017, was Election Day. We drove people to vote and tried to persuade people up until the very last minute before the polls closed. And we won. In the end, we earned 51.3 percent of the vote. My opponent earned 48.2 percent.

That night, my girls were so excited. I was so excited. I told my supporters, "All these experiences I've had, I've turned into blessings." And that's true. Those setbacks have made me stronger and have made me able to serve better. After all, it's a whole lot easier to serve people when you're not judging them.

When I was sworn in on January 8, 2018, I asked for a poem to be read. It's a poem titled "What You Allow, Lingers" by Annette Hope Billings, a Topeka native whom we like to call the Maya Angelou of the Midwest:

What you allow, lingers,
what you invite, stays put,

so speak rudely to discord
and its sullen sisters,
turn a cold shoulder to bigotry
in all its disguises,
ignore the doorbell when jealousy rings,
and stop violence at the door—like a stranger.
usher in joy like a long lost friend—
take its coat, its hat,
entertain peace,
chat up passion,
pamper generosity,
give the guest room to justice.
Sweep the porch
and place a welcome mat for goodness,
make your life poorly-suited
for anything but love.
and when hate knocks, act like you've moved!

I had to shut down and shut out a lot of bad in my life, but I was able to welcome in a lot of good, too. And here I am, the first Latina mayor of Topeka, Kansas, with this once-in-a-lifetime opportunity to make changes that help people. I'm ready, and I'm determined to do just that.

ANDREW GILLUM

Governor // Florida // Candidate in 2018

MY FIRST CAMPAIGN CAME WHEN I was in middle school. I really wanted to get Doritos into our school's vending machines, and I was passionately committed to that goal. But, sadly, we fell short.

That loss started my political career, but I didn't quit there.

When I was a student at Florida A&M University, then-governor Jeb Bush was firmly set on removing affirmative action from Florida's higher education admissions process. He had campaigned on education reform and school vouchers, but instead of sticking to those programs, he sprang "One Florida," his executive order ending affirmative action, on the public.

The outcry was palpable, and it should have been—his decisions had strong political overtones with his brother running for president. The fact that someone could play politics with a decision that so deeply affected people like me—the fifth of seven African American children born to a mother who was a bus driver and a father who was a construction worker— was incredibly disheartening.

But his decision struck a chord with me. It became as plain as day that elections have consequences and that if people were not sitting at the table, then they were very likely to be on the menu.

I resolved that Jeb Bush's decision would be the last time I was ever on the menu.

In 2003 I decided to run for the Tallahassee City Commission, a five-member board with a multimillion-dollar budget, which makes decisions that affect hundreds of thousands of constituents and carries on its shoulders the reputation of our state's capital city.

I didn't have the most money in that campaign, and I definitely wasn't the favorite to win. But we ran a campaign that spoke unapologetically to our constituents—including college students. When you want to represent Tallahassee, home of two of Florida's leading universities, you have to speak to student issues. Even though they had typically not made up a large portion of voters, I was determined to make sure their voices were heard in our government. We signed up our friends as volunteers, and we handed out T-shirts to strangers. We hit the pavement, and we hit it hard.

When we made the runoff for that City Commission seat, we worked even harder. I was not born into a political family, and I didn't have an electoral machine ready to work for me. All I had were my family, my friends, my faith, and the community I wanted to represent. And in the end, I had 57 percent of the vote in our runoff election, making me the youngest person ever elected to the Tallahassee City Commission. A decade later, I was elected mayor.

Looking back, it was an audacious vote of confidence from the people of Tallahassee to give the keys of a city like Tallahassee to a twenty-three-year-old. When you're on the outside looking in, you can't always understand the size, scope, and complexity of the government—and over the years, I came to find out that that challenge wasn't unique to me as a young elected official. I knew that if I was facing these challenges, surely my peers around the country were facing the same headwinds in their cities, counties, and states.

Thus began the Young Elected Officials Network as part of People For the American Way. PFAW, as it's known, works on civic engagement and good governance programs across the country. I worked for them during my time on the City Commission, and I led the YEO Network as national director to help train and support young progressive officials around the country.

ELECTIONS
★ HAVE ★
CONSEQUENCES

We knew that there are obstacles to getting young people elected. They're usually underfunded relative to their competitors, and they're rarely as well known as older candidates who have had opportunities to build their networks.

But another, less-talked-about challenge that I faced head-on in my own city included the difficulties of governing. I realized that not only did we need to empower and teach young people to run for office; we also needed to train them how to serve. After all, there's no point in electing young people to office if they're not able to successfully do the job.

The YEO Network helped tackle that problem all around America. From tiny towns that you've probably never heard of to midsize and large cities, the YEO Network began to take shape.

Today, I'm proud to say that we have trained some of the most dynamic, exciting, and forward-thinking elected officials in our nation.

From Georgia House of Representatives Minority Leader and gubernatorial candidate Stacey Abrams, to Arizona Congresswoman and U.S. Senator Kyrsten Sinema, to former Obama Housing and Urban Development Secretary Julián Castro and his twin brother, Congressman Joaquin Castro, the YEO Network has produced well-known elected officials and candidates running for some of the highest offices in the land.

But we've also trained candidates who are the groundbreaking leaders of tomorrow—leaders such as Rashida Tlaib, a Muslim American who was elected to the U.S. House of Representatives in Michigan; Peggy Flanagan, a Native American who was elected as Minnesota's lieutenant governor; Faith Winter, who was elected to Colorado's state senate; and Daniel Hernández Jr., who saved Gabby Giffords's life and won his election as a state representative in Arizona.

These young elected officials represent the rich diversity of our country not just in their ethnicities and skin colors but in their ages and ideas. They're putting forward the kinds of diverse, innovative ideas that show just how much progress can be made when you put yourself out there and run for office.

I first ran for office seeking neither the spotlight nor any accolades. I ran to make a difference and to make sure that my communities had a voice in their government. That's how I won their confidence and their votes.

When I decided to run to become the governor of Florida, I knew the odds were stacked against me. I didn't have a famous last name, the ability to write my own check, or all the big-name endorsements. But I knew that the twenty million people I wanted to represent were calling out for a voice in their government.

Their issues are the issues I grew up with as a kid in Miami and Gainesville. Too many of our families say they struggle to make ends meet. Our state has suffered two of the worst mass shootings in American history. Our public schools are a mess—thanks to Jeb Bush, who first pushed privatization of the public school system when I started this journey.

As I made my way around this state—home to ten media markets, two time zones, and more highways than most countries—I asked everyone for the same thing I asked for back in 2003:

A chance to be their voice.

NELSON ARAUJO

Secretary of State // Nevada // Candidate in 2018

GROWING UP, I REMEMBER hanging out at our local laundromat on Sundays. Some of my fondest memories were created during the hours-long wait for Mom to wash our laundry loads.

For Mom, it was another day of making ends meet. For me and my sister, it was an adventure—an adventure that often included us going from machine to machine looking for any quarters accidentally left behind. If we were lucky to find a few, we would use those quarters to play a video game or score a bubble gum ball.

The laundromat was just one block over from where we lived, on Twenty-Eighth Street in Las Vegas. Back then, Twenty-Eighth Street had a notoriety that could only be matched by areas like Naked City or other pockets of town plagued with gangs and violence. But for me, those streets were home. Those streets were where my mom, a single parent who'd fled the civil war in El Salvador, provided shelter for her family. Those streets were where she raised her children, where she raised me.

At a young age, I recognized the added barriers that kids like me faced. I struggled to find my lane. I struggled to envision who and what I could become. My aspirations felt like unattainable dreams.

There were loved ones, mentors, and community leaders who pushed me to accept that I could be the best me—folks who picked me up at my lowest points in life, folks who saw something in me that I refused to see, folks who pushed me to work harder at every step of the way.

But there was one specific night that inspired me to avoid the path of least resistance and to take the direction in life that led me to where I am today.

I was in grade school at the time, and my mom had just arrived home from working a long shift of cleaning hotel rooms. She always had something for my sister and me: Sometimes it was groceries, sometimes it was stuff that hotel guests had left behind weeks back and the time allotted for someone to return and claim it had finally passed, but our favorite was when she would sneak a pineapple cheesecake from the hotel's employee dining room. She could have gotten in trouble, but she knew how much my sister and I loved it, so for her it was a risk worth taking.

My mom was always tired, but this evening was different. She was exhausted. She felt defeated. The chemicals she had to use at work would make her hands peel. New management had come in, and they were inspecting the rooms with gloves, and any spot of dust could get her written up, which meant that Mom would be one step closer to being fired, so she scrubbed toilets and bathtubs on her knees, sometimes with cleaning supplies that she would buy herself because they worked better.

She looked around the house, saw the mess that my sister and I had created, and broke down. Feeling hopeless, she looked at us with tears in her eyes and said:

"Todos mis sacrificios son para que ustedes puedan vivir la vida que yo no pude."

"All of my sacrifices are so that you two can live the life that I couldn't."

That vivid memory still haunts me to this day, and since that moment I have been on a personal quest to be a voice for everyday Nevadans like my mom, a single parent who fled a war-torn country and settled in a foreign land with a language she didn't know, starting from scratch, all to make sure her kids had a shot at the American dream.

There are people like my mom throughout Nevada. And at age twenty-six, I decided to run for the Nevada assembly to stand up for them. The path to victory was not easy: I was a young, gay Latino with very little money, almost no name recognition, and little experience on a campaign trail. But I had a burning desire to help lift up my community. Despite the obstacles, my family and friends carried me across the finish line, and, thanks to them, I became the first openly gay Latino elected in Nevada and the youngest member of the Nevada legislature during the Seventy-Eighth legislative session.

There's something incredible about going back into the community that gave you so much and knowing that you are working toward improving the lives of its people. I get to return to my stomping grounds and tell students in grade school that they can be all they want to be in life, regardless of the cards that life has dealt them. That's pretty great. Especially since I have to remind myself every day that I deserve to be where I am, and that kids like me do have a place in positions of power.

I'm proud of the work my colleagues and I accomplished in the Nevada legislature during my two terms. In 2015, we were in the minority, but still, we blocked terrible proposals like one that would have essentially segregated our transgender youth in public schools. We blocked endless efforts to allow guns in schools and egregious attempts to remove well-deserved rights and benefits from Nevadans. In 2017, we won back the majority. And, while I was serving as assistant majority leader, we led incredible efforts to create jobs, invest in clean energy, and pass legislation that would protect our most vulnerable communities.

Serving in the Nevada legislature was both an honor and a privilege, but given the constant threats to our democracy and our elections, in September 2017, I launched my bid to become Nevada's next secretary of state. When I announced my candidacy, I said, "People fought and died for our right to vote in free and accessible elections . . . I believe an open government depends on fair elections and that will be my guiding principle in office."

So why do I run?

I run to protect and preserve our most fundamental right as Americans: the right to vote.

I run to lift the voices of everyday Nevadans who are desperately asking for a government that works for them and not against them.

I run so that kids who grew up on streets similar to Twenty-Eighth Street know that, for kids like us, the path to success is harder but so much more rewarding in the end.

Most important, I run to make sure that folks like my mom are at the forefront of every political conversation. After all, my mom's story is not unique. In every part of this great nation, we find stories similar to hers, and we have a responsibility—a moral obligation—to do all we can to fight for these people.

That's why I run.

★ I RUN TO ★

PROTECT

 AND

PRESERVE

OUR MOST

FUNDAMENTAL RIGHT

AS AMERICANS:

THE RIGHT TO

VOTE

JENNY DURKAN

Mayor // Seattle, Washington // Elected in 2017

NOVEMBER 9, 2016.

Waking up the day after the election was disorienting. We went from the president of hope to the complete opposite.

When Donald Trump was elected, the world started spinning differently for me.

Like so many others, my first inclination was to resist. I marched with millions across the country to speak out against his divisive actions and his assaults on dignity, equality, and democracy. I had a thousand bumper stickers printed with one word: *resist*.

Then, a week after his inauguration, President Trump issued his unconstitutional executive order banning Muslims from entering the United States. It was clear that resisting alone would not be enough.

As a former U.S. attorney, I could not stand on the sidelines.

Within minutes, I was on the phone with a key port authority commissioner, who oversees Seattle-Tacoma International Airport. I drove there right away. In the car, speeding down the freeway, I called the best civil rights and immigration attorneys I knew in Seattle. They, too, were mobilizing people to go to the airport, ready to work together to stand up for the rule of law.

At the airport, it was a chaotic scene: Port officials and our growing army of volunteer lawyers had little information. People were arriving from all over the world to see family, to journey to other places, to move to our country, or to just come home. But unlike on any other day, some were being turned away because of their religious beliefs. Talking with families awaiting the arrival of their loved ones, we learned that a number of people were unable to make it through customs despite having proper travel documents. As time ticked away, we learned that two men who had been detained were being placed on a flight to be sent "back home."

Our team went into high gear to get a court order as the men were placed on the plane. It was a race against time as we worked to stop the plane, which was pulling away from the jet bridge.

Seattle's best legal minds quickly wrote and filed one of the first motions in the country requesting a court injunction to help prevent their deportations. Even on a Saturday, we got the pleadings filed and found a judge to read and rule almost immediately—which was no easy feat. With the order in hand, the jet was stopped and the men brought back. I could not have been prouder of our work and of the strength of our independent federal courts.

While we ultimately succeeded in stopping the deportation of those arriving in Seattle, that day brought a renewed realization that the Trump presidency was dangerous and a threat to our values and our future.

Too many Americans suddenly had to worry if they would continue to have a home in our country.

* * *

President Trump's vision for America is built on unpredictability and fueling dissension. He uses bullying and chaos to divide and theatrics to distract. He constantly tries to move the boundary of decency. He stands against everything Seattle stands for.

In Seattle, we believe that every person is born with dignity and promise and deserves respect and real opportunity—that a person's value is not based on net worth, country of birth, skin color, or sexual orientation. We believe we are all better off when prosperity is shared and is not just reserved for the few. And we know that we are stronger, more innovative, and more successful when we are a truly inclusive place.

I had the honor of serving under President Obama for years. My children met him and were inspired by him. He urged them to make the world better. I knew I couldn't let Trump's values stand as the values of America. I could not let them determine the world my children will one day inherit. We are so much better than that.

Seattle is strong, resilient, determined, generous, and—frankly—the best damn city anywhere. I wanted to be part of showing the rest of the country what it looks like when a city turns its progressive values into action.

So in May 2017, I decided to run for mayor.

I had worked in and out of government in Seattle for years, but I'd never run for office before. Still, I knew, in this moment, that we could not look to Washington, D.C., for a better world. Leadership would come from local government. If I wanted to help lead the way forward, I needed to step up. For my city. For my country. For my kids. I wanted them to know—and all young people to know—that, even when it might not seem like it, government can be a force for good in people's lives.

* * *

Throughout my life, I've been privileged to be in positions that helped me be that force for good.

After college I spent two years as a volunteer teacher and basketball coach in a remote Alaskan village. I was there to teach, but I ended up being the one who learned so much—from my students and from the villagers, particularly from the Native American elders who opened their homes and families to me.

During law school, I volunteered in a prison counseling project that took me inside a local prison on a semi-regular basis. Seeing life on the inside was eye-opening. Nothing prepares you for the first time the prison door clangs shut behind you—locking you in. Instinctively, you stop in your tracks and search for the face that will make sure you really can get out again.

I got my first courtroom experience through a criminal defense clinic in law school, where I worked with the public defender's office representing clients in Seattle Municipal Court.

After law school, I represented people in the worst of circumstances— such as the family of a firefighter who died in a warehouse fire and a woman denied the right to see her partner in the hospital after a flash flood. I was fortunate to represent people in cases with broader impacts, but, as a lawyer, you're usually tilting windmills one at a time. I fought for changes to make the system better.

When President Barack Obama appointed me U.S. attorney for the Western District of Washington, I learned more about the positive impact you can have within the system itself, especially working for the Justice Department—the only federal agency with a moral value in its name. I worked with communities throughout western Washington to reduce crime. We targeted gun crimes, cyber criminals, and large drug cartels to make our region safer. Enforcement is essential to public safety, but so are prevention and redemption. During my career, I worked with other leaders to come up with alternatives to incarceration by creating local and federal drug courts and a mental health court. I also partnered with community groups to investigate and reform the Seattle Police Department. I created a civil rights unit within our office to focus on housing discrimination, job discrimination, and the rights of returning veterans.

Being U.S. attorney was an incredible job. When I left, I moved back to private practice as global chair of a cybersecurity and data protection practice in an international law firm. It, too, was a great job.

★ ★ ★

In May 2017, I was running for a new kind of job: mayor of Seattle. I was also running my first campaign. It was a whirlwind. After my announcement, it was a flurry of media interviews, neighborhood walks, and community meetings to listen to voters. I loved getting to know new people and seeing the city that I loved from a new perspective.

But the most important thing I heard during the campaign was that people in Seattle were yearning for our city to push for progress and not let our president take us backward. And, in particular, they were looking for a woman to lead. Even in one of the most progressive cities in the country, the last female mayor had served nearly a century earlier.

I laid out my vision for our city and my priorities: two years of free community college for Seattle Public Schools graduates; housing assistance for families struggling with our affordability and homelessness crisis;

leadership on climate change; deliberate action to address economic and racial disparities. I pledged to bring people together to show our progressive values at work. And I committed to standing up for our values in the face of attacks from what I call the "other Washington."

I will always be grateful that my neighbors in Seattle placed their trust in me to make those pledges real.

Seattle is now run by women at every level of government. Our city council has a supermajority of both women and people of color. I appointed our first woman of color as chief of police. Having women in leadership positions leads to a different style of governance. It also has a society-changing effect. It helps every little girl know that she can be whatever she wants—and every little boy, too.

After the "Year of the Woman" in 1992, I heard a speaker who said that the first people who break the glass ceiling are going to get a lot of cuts. There were so many women before me who were willing to break those barriers, knowing the price they might pay. Women such as Ann Richards and Christine Gregoire, Barbara Jordan and Patty Murray, Hillary Clinton and Sandra Day O'Connor all stepped up at a time when it was even harder for women to win public office.

And while women continue to get cuts, some deeper than others, it feels as if healing is starting to happen. Women are stepping up and running for office at record levels.

It's about time.

ANDREA JENKINS

City Council // Minneapolis, Minnesota // Elected in 2017

★

MY WHOLE LIFE, I HAVE served my community. I have seen how policy impacts people's lives.

My first job was with Junior Achievement of the Upper Midwest. I worked as a Business Basics recruiter. I recruited volunteers to go into fifth- and sixth-grade classrooms to teach Business Basics once a week. One of my recruits was Jackie Cherryhomes. She was the president of the Minneapolis City Council at the time. She thought it was critical for young people to meet adults in leadership roles, and I thought it was inspiring to see political leaders, like Jackie, engaged with their community.

My next job was as a counselor at a chemical dependency treatment center. I helped people—mostly people of color—find employment as they worked to overcome addiction. This was in the early 1990s. The crack epidemic was in full swing in Minneapolis. There was no shortage of people to work with. Many of my clients were also dealing with unjust minimum sentencing standards.

I saw how these blanket policies contributed to the ongoing inequities in our society. I saw how these policies led to America becoming the world's most incarcerated country, per capita. I saw how they could tear families apart—not just my clients' families but my own. My little brother fell victim to crack cocaine addiction and was imprisoned and then died from the ravages he experienced. (Of course, now we are seeing something different happening with drug policy. With the opioid epidemic, an epidemic that impacts more white families, the conversation has shifted from incarceration to compassion.)

After that, I worked with Hennepin County, where I was a counselor for mothers and families receiving public assistance. In 1996, the Clinton administration passed the Welfare Reform Act, and the amount of time a family could receive federal cash assistance was limited to five years. Again, I saw how policy could put a heavy burden on people—in this case, women and children.

Policy can have a big impact on people's lives. It certainly has had one on mine, as I came to terms with my gender identity.

From a very young age, I felt different. But I also felt the societal pressure to conform to the ideals of masculinity. So I tried—rather successfully, I might add—to go along. I played football in high school. I joined a fraternity in college. I got married and fathered a beautiful daughter.

However, the internal struggle to be one's true self is powerful. I came out to my family as bisexual, but that was not the full truth. I wanted to be fully authentic with myself and with those I loved.

And it turned out that my city, Minneapolis, was a pretty good place to do that. Minneapolis was actually the first city in the country to pass protections for transgender people.

So, five years into working with the county, I came out as a transgender woman. This was one of the most liberating experiences of my life. I joined several nonprofit organizations, at first as a way to ensure that I had allies if I ever needed them. But, after a while, I found that the more I fought to improve the lives of others, the more I was improving life for myself.

I worked with the county for another five years after that. Coming to terms with my true self allowed me to flourish in ways I hadn't been able to before. I wanted to do more to improve people's lives. So I finished my undergraduate degree, a degree that I had started twenty years earlier. I went on to obtain a graduate degree in community economic development.

After I graduated, I attended a community leadership institute at the University of St. Thomas. There, I met Robert Lilligren, who was running for city council. When he won his seat, he appointed me to serve as his senior policy aide in city hall. That's how I started working in politics and seeing how you could improve people's lives through elected office. I went on to serve in this role for two subsequent city council members for a total of twelve years.

Doing this work, I learned the rigors of elected office and the fortitude required in the fight for equity and full equality for all people. I also learned that if you want to be effective, you have to be broad-based and intersectional. Robert identifies as a Native American and a gay man, but that never defined how he governed; rather, it informed his decision-making.

In 2016, when my former boss decided not to seek reelection, I started to think about running for office myself. I attended campaign training through the Victory Fund, a group that teaches LGBTQ people how to run for office. And I pulled together an amazing group of activists, community leaders, and politicos—who, by the way, were almost all women. We put together a campaign plan.

I was already planning to run when America elected a reality-TV star to be president. But his election gave me extra incentive. I knew that cities were going to become the center of political change in our society, and I knew that I wanted to be a part of that change.

A couple of community members organized a "RUN ANDREA RUN" campaign on Facebook, too. It got more than five hundred "likes" and comments encouraging me to run. It was clear that people needed someone to believe in in light of the 2016 election. So I announced I was running a month before Donald Trump was sworn into office.

For the first five months of my campaign, we did not have an opponent, at least not a personal one. But I told my team that we were always running against the opponents racism, sexism, and transphobia.

We saw those opponents at work, in little ways, on the campaign trail. At one event, a person assumed that I must be running in the ward representing the predominantly black community on the Northside. In fact, I was running to represent a more diverse community on the Southside. Another time, a person asked me bluntly, "How do you handle door knocking as a black transgender person?"

I KNEW THAT
CITIES
WERE GOING TO BECOME
★★★ THE CENTER OF ★★★
POLITICAL CHANGE
IN OUR SOCIETY,
AND I KNEW THAT I WANTED
TO BE A PART OF THAT
 CHANGE

Facing things like that, I knew that we needed to run a campaign that was focused on the issues—and the policies—that impact the lives of the people in the Eighth Ward and throughout Minneapolis. We hosted our own community forums. We showed up at community events. We went to neighborhood meetings, parades, ice cream socials—you name it. We made thousands of phone calls and knocked on hundreds of doors. We worked hard to reach every voter.

We especially wanted to reach people who weren't likely to show up to vote—folks who have been historically shut out of the electoral process. We wanted to engage young people of color who had never voted before. We wanted to engage the immigrant community, the transgender community, and the broader LGBTQ community.

All that work paid off. We increased voter turnout, and we won the seat with 73 percent of the vote.

It still blows my mind to this day. But, to me, it says that people want change. They want rights for immigrants, people with disabilities, and LGBTQ people. They want women's rights and reproductive rights. They believe that Black Lives Matter. They want to see everyone treated as equal human beings. They want everyone's lives to be better.

I have seen how policy impacts people's lives. Politics, too. The late senator from Minnesota Paul Wellstone said, "Politics is about improving people's lives."

That's why I ran. That's why I serve.

KAREN CAUDILLO

DACA Recipient // Senior at the University of Central Florida //
Aspiring Candidate

★

MY ENTIRE BODY SHOOK with heartbreak and anger as I watched Attorney General Jeff Sessions announce an end to the Deferred Action for Childhood Arrivals (DACA) program. I knew that the administration wanted to get rid of the program, which offers protections and opportunities for people like me who immigrated to this country as children. They made it pretty clear through hateful tweets and campaign trail taunts.

Still, the morning of the announcement, I felt unprepared. I felt disheartened—after all that time and effort I'd dedicated to doing well in school, all my family's hard work in houses and restaurants and on construction sites. They'd worked day in and day out so that I could have a better life. This was our home, but we were being told to get out.

A few days after that, on my way to class, I saw two young white guys asking other students for their signatures. They were working to win a seat in our university's student senate.

A light bulb turned on in my head. If they can do it, why can't I?

I immigrated to the United States from Mexico with my parents at the age of four. My parents put their lives on the line for me. We were undocumented. But they saw that poverty, crime, instability, and scarce opportunities in higher education, especially for women, would hold me back. So they set their sights on Naples, Florida.

When I was in kindergarten, my school assigned me a tutor who would visit me twice a week at home. A couple of years later, after becoming fluent in English, I was put in the gifted program at my elementary school.

While I was in middle school, my family temporarily moved from our predominantly white, small hometown of Naples to diverse, bustling Los Angeles. It was a complete culture shock. My new classmates were proud Asian, black, and Chicano students, but they were treated differently. They were living a different reality than white people.

I thought returning to Naples would make me feel safer, but it turned out to be the opposite. We returned to Naples as I started high school—and people in my community started to disappear. I didn't know it at the time, but the county had started a voluntary program, with support from the federal government, that allowed close collaboration between local police and Immigration and Customs Enforcement (ICE) deportation agents. It was called a 287(g) program.

My father organized salsa and cumbia events for our community. There is a video of five thousand people participating in the largest event he ever hosted. Watching it today, I can point out every friend who was detained or deported because of the 287(g) program—fathers, mothers, sisters, brothers who never returned home.

When I got my first cell phone, I never let its battery die. I was so afraid that my mom or dad could be next. I worried about my family being torn apart. I worried about being undocumented. I worried about getting into college. All that worry was a heavier weight than the books in my backpack.

But I kept pushing forward and holding out hope.

Halfway through my time in high school, immigrant youth and adults across the country successfully pressured President Barack Obama to announce the DACA policy. I qualified for the program.

After that, one of my teachers helped me get TheDream.US scholarship, a private scholarship designed for DACA recipients at select schools. Miami Dade College was one of those schools. It was two hours away from

THERE COMES

◄ A ►

POINT WHEN

YOU JUST CAN'T BE

AFRAID

★ ANYMORE ★

home and not my first choice, but I wasn't about to turn down the opportunity. I got in. Everything seemed to fall into place.

I commuted to Miami Dade College. Every Tuesday and Thursday, I would drive two hours there and two hours back, with twelve hours of classes and studying in between. After a year and a half, I walked across the stage with my associate's degree in hand, becoming the first in my family to graduate with a degree. My parents cried when they saw me. This was their dream.

I was accepted into the University of Central Florida (UCF) as a transfer student. I was excited to start my studies in political science. I was excited to create change, to create a world where we left things even better than we received them—whether that's expanding access to higher education, preserving and sustaining our land and water, or crafting policies that allow immigrants and communities of color to thrive.

I felt like I was on the cusp of a breakthrough. My passions kept building. And then DACA was terminated. Suddenly, all my plans came crashing down.

But there comes a point when you just can't be afraid anymore.

When I saw the two young white men running for the university's student senate, I knew I had to give it a shot. Couldn't a woman of color lead? Why not me?

Between labor club meetings and political theory classes, I launched my campaign. I gathered signatures. And pretty soon I was elected as a senator for the College of Sciences, representing a thousand students.

Around that same time, I went to a Defend DACA rally in Orlando. There, I met activists from For Our Future and the Farmworker Association of Florida. They asked me if I wanted to go to Washington, D.C., and take part in a hunger strike to protest the decision to end DACA and call on Congress to pass the DREAM Act. Without a doubt in my mind, I said yes.

Everyone wanted to know what immigrant youth were going to do now that our opportunities were being stripped away from us and what we were willing to risk to win back our lives.

I stepped out of the shadows when reporters from the *Guardian* and the *New York Times* interviewed me during the hunger strike. After that, conservative bloggers called me a fraud. Hateful trolls added their comments to the mix. But what scared me most was that my home address got out there. All I could think about was my parents' safety.

Nonetheless, my family supported me. I kept going back to Washington. I chanted my lungs out. I posted photos and videos online. I visited dozens of congressional offices to share my story and even held a sit-in at the office of my own senator.

The Trump administration and Congress failed to act. It was heartbreaking. But, still, I was filled with pride. I'd stood up for myself, for my family.

When I returned to school at UCF, I decided to build on that momentum, and I ran for student body president with another woman as my running mate. We knew the race would be tough: Leadership at my school has historically been dominated by white men, and women of color and undocumented youth have been afforded few opportunities for a seat at the table. It was time to make herstory.

By running, I made people like me visible. My campaign pushed a grassroots, progressive platform that spoke to the issues and people our school had overlooked. We highlighted university-wide sustainability practices, support systems for sexual-assault survivors, and awareness of our undocumented youth student population. My biggest opponent was also undocumented, but he was more hesitant to own his story.

Ultimately, I lost in the runoff election but not without sharing my truth.

No matter if a campaign ends in a win or a loss, the work must continue. As a young immigrant, as a woman of color, I know that I have to trust my heart and my vision because I've witnessed the transformation our communities can create when we are empowered to overcome the shame and fear society forces upon us. As I approach graduation, I continue to look toward the future. I want to run for office. I want to lead.

Today, I look at the members of Congress who failed to pass the DREAM Act. I know there will be a day when we will push them to pass the bill, to provide us a path to citizenship, to make it so I can run for office. One day, I will fill their shoes and, as an elected official, I will proudly and joyfully fight for those whose voices aren't heard. I will disrupt business as usual. And I will pass laws that transform my hometown, my state, and my country for the better.

TOM PERRIELLO

Governor // Virginia // Candidate in 2017

ON NOVEMBER 5, 2013, my home state of Virginia was in the process of electing new leaders. A year earlier, I almost entered the race as a candidate for governor. But instead, on Election Day, I was seven thousand miles away, knee-deep in water on a flooded Afghanistan street, leaving an all-night session with Pashtun warlords talking about their country's chance to have what we take for granted—a peaceful, democratic transfer of power.

As dawn was about to break, with polls closing back home, I was certain: This was where I was supposed to be.

Service can take a thousand forms—teaching, healing, performing, running for office, parenting, serving in the military or the diplomatic corps. Answering the call to serve has taken me into the Oval Office for meetings with President Barack Obama and into attack helicopters doing banking turns inside the mouth of a volcano in eastern Congo. I have snuck war crime indictments against brutal dictators across borders and been spit on while protesting neo-Nazis in my hometown of Charlottesville. I have been blessed to work with some of the most courageous and inspiring youth leaders around the world and even helped a few get released from prison. Not long before my father passed away, he got to see me elected to Congress, and I got to cast a deciding vote that provided better health care to tens of millions of Americans.

The call to serve can take you just about anywhere, but only if you answer it.

* * *

For me, this series of very different missions to serve began from a simple but powerful place—guilt. My earliest childhood memories feature an all-you-can-eat buffet of Catholic guilt, white guilt, Southern guilt, class guilt, male guilt, "perfect home" guilt.

Every day of my childhood began with a journey that crossed the lines of American inequality. It was my bus route. It began in our small neighborhood with a half dozen white kids, the children of doctors and bankers, waiting at the bottom of long driveways leading to tucked-away but expansive homes. Then the bus crossed the railroad tracks—less than half a mile away but a different world—where every kid was African American, and some of the houses and trailers were barely standing. We would joke, sing, sometimes even hold hands across these divides, but every kid was smart enough to see that life had not dealt everyone the same hand, particularly when stories of summer camps or Christmas gifts were in season.

That was nothing compared to the divides once we got to school. I can hardly remember a time before teachers were telling me I could be president some day—or before noticing that teachers were encouraging kids from the other side of the tracks to aim for very different futures. According to family lore, by the age of five I began asking what it would take to make sure every kid had the same chances.

The answer required divine inspiration. As a deeply religious kid, I came of age in a Catholic community that reserved a special place in hell for those who turned a blind eye to human suffering, poverty, and torture. I heard sermons about how charity was necessary but not sufficient to meet Christ's demand for us to overturn unjust and dehumanizing structures like the tables of corrupt moneylenders at the Temple. I heard stories about courageous nuns in El Salvador who had been raped and killed by right-wing militias supported by our own government merely for standing with the poor. During those formative years, the Gospel's message—"We shall be known by our deeds"—was carved indelibly into my heart.

When it comes to a life of service, I signed up for the guilt but stayed for the joy. Guilt is powerful, but it can also corrode the soul. While I remain forever indebted to Catholic theology for pushing me into this life, it took me years to overcome a sometimes toxic sense of martyrdom and admit that I love this work, this calling. I love the inspiring, courageous people it has allowed me to meet, work with, and learn from. I love that, no matter how depressed I get, I am surrounded by people who have survived far worse and still believe the arc of history bends toward justice.

I have won elections and lost elections. I have been part of successful peace negotiations and ones that failed with horrific consequences. I have known courageous human rights leaders who have become elected leaders and some who were murdered or still suffer in prison.

Sometimes the work is dramatic or even risky—the projects my nieces and nephews think are cool—while other times, making the most difference required painstaking work inside a bureaucracy to write the Quadrennial Diplomacy and Development Review to help the Obama administration modernize the way America engages with the rest of the world.

I have opted to change jobs every year or two, testing different theories of what makes a difference in the world. I have tried, since turning eighteen, to choose each mission based on where I can make the most difference at that time, not down the road. I have a bias for the jobs and missions other people don't want or think are impossible to win. I've had to muster a high willingness to fail—aware that this is an opportunity and perhaps even an obligation afforded me by the privileges of being an Ivy League–educated white male in America whom society gives room to "fail upward."

* * *

As I look back, few decision points shaped my life more than the choice, right after law school, to move to Sierra Leone to teach and to support a flailing peace process. At that time, the West African country ranked dead last on the United Nations "misery index" that measures factors such as literacy, poverty, disease, and life expectancy (a shocking thirty-four years old at the time). For nearly a decade, brutal rebel groups had committed unspeakable atrocities, often carried out by child soldiers who had themselves been abducted, drugged, and forced to do terrible things to their own family members so that they would never be welcomed back to their own villages.

Sierra Leone had been written off as a hopeless hell on earth by most observers. But a group of local women leaders refused to accept that fate. During a trip I took there during law school, the bravest of them all, Zainab Bangura, pitched me on moving there to help them end the civil war with a just peace. I asked what my value would be as an outsider, and she replied, "If you are standing next to me, I am a lot less likely to be shot, and that would be very valuable to me."

Enough said.

Over the next two years, I watched and worked with these bold women as they demanded and got a peace agreement. They demanded and delivered justice, including the arrests of powerful and vicious leaders who remain in jail today. Some of the breakthroughs were dramatic and came with risks, while others came from the tireless, thankless research of my students developing a credible methodology for running the country's first public opinion poll. Their exhausting, creative academic work helped break the long deadlock at the peace talks.

The civil war that people predicted would never end has not restarted in more than fifteen years. When the Ebola crisis was waning in the region years later, one of the leading activists said to me, "Imagine how many hundreds of thousands might be dead if we were still fighting, if we had listened to everyone who said peace was impossible." These women taught me that true leadership is not defined by titles but rather by a fearless willingness to change our sense of the possible. While those in power focus on claiming credit and making excuses, change movements—often led by young people— transform what we have too long treated as inevitable into the unacceptable.

I remember years later, when I was in Congress, how strange it felt when people and pundits gave me credit for casting "courageous" votes on health care, climate change, and immigration reform that would likely cost me my seat in a deeply conservative district. I certainly appreciated the kinds words—I will never forget watching President Obama give me

THE CALL TO

SERVE

CAN TAKE YOU JUST ABOUT

ANYWHERE

★ BUT ONLY IF YOU ★

ANSWER IT

a shout-out on *The Daily Show*!—but I remember thinking that we have set the bar for political courage way too low. The worst thing that might happen to me is losing an election, and there are a lot worse fates in life than being a former member of Congress. Casting those principled votes may have cost me my seat, but they also helped create new opportunities to run one of the most important national progressive groups and later serve as an appointee of President Obama. When it comes to following your convictions, when one door closes, another one opens.

* * *

This sense of calling became a sonic boom with President Donald Trump's election, and I announced my campaign for governor of Virginia. Twenty years of fighting uphill battles for justice alongside inspiring leaders allowed me to dare to believe that this cataclysmic presidency could be transformed into a catalyst—a catalyst for bolder progressive reform than Democrats had dared to touch for too long. While many leading Democrats were offering President Trump olive branches, I believed my campaign could set the tone in our commonwealth and country both of fierce, principled resistance to hate and of proactive demands for bold progressive reform. We lost the primary, but we elevated and mainstreamed conversations about President Trump's racism, about debt-free community college, a living wage, and criminal justice reform.

And again, a principled loss opened a new door—a chance once again to help a bold set of women reformers change the course of a country's history. I was hired as CEO of WinVirginia, an innovative effort that dared to believe Democrats could flip Virginia's House of Delegates when almost no pundit or party leader considered that possible. I got to be in the political trenches with dozens of inspiring candidates—brilliant, bold leaders like Danica Roem and Debra Rodman, Jennifer Carroll Foy and Elizabeth Guzmán—who answered the call to enter the political arena against the odds to resist, persist, and reclaim the promise of an inclusive Virginia. On Election Night of 2017, we celebrated as Virginia elected the most women delegates in its history—including the first two Latina delegates, the first two Asian American women delegates, the first transgender delegate (and former investigative journalist), and the first public defender.

The results we produced together in Virginia in 2017 created shock waves that are reverberating across the country. Progressives exhausted by the daily assaults from the Trump administration began to believe that victory was not just possible but within reach. Candidates in red states and districts could cite the Virginia delegates as Exhibit A in their case that the utterly improbable was indeed possible. That we could imagine a Democratic senator from Alabama and a progressive majority in "the people's House."

From crossing the railroad tracks to crisscrossing the world, a journey originally fueled by guilt is now propelled by the joy and impacts I have been blessed to experience. Everyone must find his or her own path, and I never know where mine might lead next. But I know that choosing the path of making the most difference now can produce some wins and some losses but never regrets and never a limit on what progress is possible.

KEVINDARYÁN LUJÁN

Orange County Legislator // New York's 4th District //
Elected in 2017

MY MOTHER AND GRANDMOTHER wanted to escape the economic hardship and political strife in Colombia. So they worked hard and came to the United States. They came, like so many, in search of the American dream.

My grandmother sold everything she owned when she came here. When my family settled in the Hudson Valley, she worked as a waitress and cleaned houses. She saved money under her mattress. And eventually she saved enough to buy a house—the first person in my family to do so. She bought a little two-family house in Newburgh, New York, a city of about thirty thousand, just west of the Hudson River. She saw the potential in Newburgh and believed that it would be a great place to raise her family. She was so proud of buying that home.

My mother left all her friends behind when she came here. She didn't speak English. That was hard for her. She was only ten at the time. She got pregnant with me when she was fifteen. That was hard, too. People told her that her life was over. But she pushed through. She graduated from

Mount Saint Mary College, the local college in Newburgh, and got a graduate degree and a law degree after that.

I was raised by strong, independent, fearless women. They encouraged me to work hard and dream big. They encouraged me to serve others. So I knew from a very young age that I wanted to help my neighbors and my friends who were in need. And later I knew that I wanted to help as many people as I could. I saved money from working part-time jobs, I applied for scholarships, and I studied abroad, in France and China and the United Arab Emirates and across Central Europe. For a child who grew up poor in the projects, this experience was truly life-changing.

In China, I learned the importance of everything from due process to freedom of speech to environmental protections. In Dubai, I witnessed the abuse of migrant workers. In Europe, I saw the negative impact of radical nationalist movements in the treatment of the Roma and Muslim communities. I learned how, sadly, history always seems to repeat itself.

I graduated from Florida International University and then from Central European University. I wanted to become a diplomat. I wanted to help improve our nation's relations with countries around the world. Yet the more I got involved in my own community, the more I realized how much good I could do in my own backyard.

I returned to my roots, to the city I had grown up in, to Newburgh, in 2012. That was where my heart was and always had been. I had seen the Great Wall of China and the Western Wall in Jerusalem, but nothing could ever compare to the view of the Hudson River from Washington's Headquarters. I wanted to give back to the community that had given so much to my family. I learned about local issues. I got involved in local politics and activism.

In 2014, Congressman Sean Patrick Maloney was up for reelection in my district, and I went to work on his campaign. It was incredible. I got to talk to community members about the problems they were facing and the concerns they had. I got to encourage young people, our communities of color, and our whole community to voice those views through voting. We worked hard on that race, and he won.

I loved that campaign. But I never really imagined running for office myself. Until one day, one year later. I woke up to the sight of thirty-seven mattresses in the backyard of the abandoned house right across the street from my grandmother's home. They sat there for two weeks, along with a sofa on our sidewalk. It was heartbreaking for my grandmother. She'd worked so hard to save money and buy a house and make it her own. And now it felt as if her neighborhood had been left behind.

I realized in that moment that my grandmother wasn't alone. There were other people in Newburgh and in other neighborhoods who were struggling. And I decided right then and there that I had to do everything I could to fight for them.

I found my voice, and I decided to run for city council. I didn't expect to win. I didn't even really know what I was doing. I worked hard to get on the ballot, only to be knocked out of the race early. I vowed never to run for office again.

I stayed involved, but I wouldn't run.

Until 2016. For me, that was a big year for two reasons.

First, my father died. When he was diagnosed with cancer, it was a devastating blow. Questions about "preexisting" conditions that had never even been on my radar suddenly switched to the forefront of my life. Without the Affordable Care Act, my father wouldn't have been able to enter hospice and live the last weeks of his life with dignity. After he died, I remembered how important life is and how short it is. I knew that I needed to make the most of each and every day.

Second, President Trump was elected. Once again, I found myself in mourning. I felt lost and abandoned in this new world order. I knew I could not watch from the sidelines. I went to meetings and rallies and marches. And the more I did, the more I knew I needed to do.

As the chaos on the national scene grew, I pushed for local solutions to protect our community. I was inspired by cities like Kingston in upstate New York, which declared itself a sanctuary city, the first in the Hudson Valley. I began working on similar resolutions in cities across the Hudson Valley, in Newburgh, Middletown, Beacon, Poughkeepsie, Woodbury, and Goshen. After a few months, many of these cities began to support the sanctuary movement, and now many of those same cities are working on municipal IDs to help undocumented immigrants access local services.

My city council voted in favor of a sanctuary city resolution I put forward in our local Democratic committee. That was one of the proudest days of my life. My eyes filled with tears of joy. I found the humanity in people that I'd feared was missing. I thought of the families in our city who were living in fear of deportation. I thought maybe this would help them sleep a little easier. And I thought if I could keep being a voice for those who lived in the shadows, then I had to do that.

So even though I had vowed never to run for office again, the thought of running began to creep in. I started by asking myself what I wanted to see in my leaders. I wanted them to be accessible, empathetic, and informed. I wanted them to use their power and their privilege to help others. I thought I could be that leader, and so I decided to run again. This time for Orange County legislator.

When I got into the race, the line between establishment Democrats and those who were against politics as usual had been drawn. But neither side seemed to welcome young people's voices. I was constantly told how entitled our generation was, or how we needed to wait our turn, or how we simply didn't understand the complexities integral to our system.

So, when creating my campaign team, I looked to those who hadn't been at the table, the young leaders in our community who believed that we could do better and dream bigger. I found true progressives in my district who had taken the time to nurture the next generation. We may not have always agreed, but we always were respectful of one another.

And on the campaign trail, I didn't shy away from my youth; I embraced it. I listened to my community—which, in the age of President Trump, seemed revolutionary. I talked about ending the status quo, about creating jobs that would provide a better future. Supporting the underrepresented—the working class, our communities of color, seniors, women, our LGBTQ community, and young people—these were the backbone of my policies. They were the backbone of my campaign, as well.

People ask me how to get young people interested in politics. I tell them: Open doors for them. Listen to them. The young people of this country have proven that the impossible can be possible. From the legalization of marijuana to commonsense gun reform to transgender rights, we are not afraid to dream big and take the steps—big and small—needed to make those dreams a reality.

The door wasn't open for my campaign team. So we created our own door and we marched through without asking for anyone's permission. We built a campaign in the image of our community—one of diversity, unity, and love. We supported one another. We dreamed with one another. We listened to the voters. We created a policy platform with their voices in mind. And after all that, we won. We did it not because it was easy but because it was hard. We recognized the importance of new energy and innovation to tackle the challenges ahead.

My campaign began with a simple question: What should our leaders look like?

Leaders should look like us. Don't let anyone tell you differently.

VI LYLES
Interviewed by Carol McDonald

Mayor // Charlotte, North Carolina // Elected in 2017

CAROL MCDONALD: What's the story of your name? I know you go by Vi, but your full name is Viola.

VI LYLES: Well, I was named after my grandmother on my father's side; her name was Viola, and whenever you're named after your family, it's a true honor. My grandmother was sassy and brassy. I think she was ninety years old and still had red hair. She was always one of those women who was regal. And I'm named after her, and my daughter is named after her, as well.

MCDONALD: Remind me, you grew up in South Carolina, is that correct?

LYLES: Yes, that's correct.

MCDONALD: Tell me a little bit about what that was like, growing up in South Carolina.

LYLES: Well, I had one of those huge families. My father grew up in Columbia, and my mother grew up in a little town outside Columbia called Hopkins. My mother had eight sisters and two brothers, and my dad had two sisters and two brothers. We are a big family, we are able to trace our roots back to slave times, and we have great family reunions.

MCDONALD: You left South Carolina to come to college in Charlotte.

LYLES: My two older brothers went to college in our hometown. I was the first one in my family to go away to college. It was at the time when colleges were being threatened with a loss of federal funding if they didn't integrate. With Lyndon Johnson and the Vietnam War, a lot was happening. My dad said, "Charlotte's close enough that if something happens, I can be there for you." He understood that the world isn't always going to be fair, and we need to be able to hang close with each other. So that's how I came to Charlotte.

MCDONALD: You went on to get your master's at Chapel Hill. What made you decide to settle back in Charlotte?

LYLES: I came out of graduate school in the middle of a very deep recession. The Public Administration program at Chapel Hill is known for placing people in local government inside the state. The men got really great jobs, but being a woman it wasn't that easy. I got a job in a little town called Salemburg, North Carolina. It had a blinking light and a cinder-block café. It was in the middle of a tobacco and cotton field, they had just opened the North Carolina Justice Academy there, and they were hiring. So I went to Salemburg, and I was there for thirty days, and I said, "This is not the place for me." A lot of black people in that town still went to the back door of the restaurant to get takeout. And when the state told the café owner that they had to serve them, they moved from ceramic plates to paper plates. So I couldn't stay, and there was a job open in Charlotte. I interviewed, got it, and there I was.

MCDONALD: You're clearly a leader now, but I wonder, did you always see yourself as a leader?

LYLES: I think we all expect to have a pretty traditional life, and I don't know that I felt like I would be in this position as a leader. I really think that I always felt that I would be able to work and would have really good friends and that we would raise our kids. It would just be a regular life.

But things change. Life doesn't always take you where you think you ought to go.

MCDONALD: How did you make the transition from civil service to running for city council?

LYLES: Well, that was a conscious decision on my part. I had worked and retired, and I started working again the day after I retired. Our city, at the time, was being considered for the Democratic National Convention in 2012, and I really believed in President Obama. I wanted to be a part of that. I sought out a position. I worked on the convention for almost two years.

During the middle of 2011, my husband was diagnosed with pancreatic cancer, and he was very, very sick. It's not an easy cancer to live with, so at the time, I said that after the convention was over, I was just going to be with him. I started staying at home. And one day, he said to me, "Vi, you've got to go find something to do; this is not you."

Anthony Foxx was our mayor, and the city was beginning to have this huge split. Anthony was saying, "We have to do things differently. We have to prove that we can be a progressive city." There were people who thought, "Well, we can't do this. We can't afford this big change." I thought, well, I've got this great skill-set on collaboration and facilitation; I'll run for office and help Anthony be successful. I really wasn't thinking about it any other way.

So I ran for office and then Anthony moved to Washington to be the secretary of transportation. And I ended up being on the city council when our next mayor got arrested for taking a bribe. And the whole experience changed.

We were very divided, and there were factions on the council. I realized that when you work in a business or even in a nonprofit, you have a common mission. And you hammer things out, but once a decision is made, and a direction is taken, everybody says, "OK, we're there."

But when you're in an elected office, people have no automatic alliance with each other. They have an alliance with the people who elected them, which is how we became so partisan. It was a real learning experience for me, because I thought truly that if you had the right people, good data, and clarity of purpose that we would all be successful. And that's not true in politics; it's just not true.

So you have to build some alliances, and I did that. Then I ran for a second term, and the council chose me as mayor pro tem. And after Lamar Scott's shooting, I decided that I would run for mayor.

MCDONALD: How did that crystallize your decision to run for mayor?

LYLES: It was the first time that I had seen Charlotte in such unrest, probably since the civil rights movement. Our city was not ready for social media protesting. We were not ready for any of it. Even though other shootings had occurred across the country, we didn't think we would go through that. It was chaotic.

I remember sitting at midnight with about forty faith leaders trying to work out how we could get ourselves to a place that we could begin to talk again versus having protests that were considered violent by some people and civil disobedience by others.

We met every morning at 6:00 A.M., trying to determine what the next steps would be. And even though it was just a few days, it seemed like a very long time. And it all culminated with a council meeting, where people came to talk about their experiences and it got heated. There were a lot of people who were really afraid on the council, but there were about four of us who said, "We're going to sit here. We're not going to walk away, because these folks are expressing how they feel."

It was probably one of the most cathartic moments in our community's history. Because people had to say something, and they had to say it to the leadership, and that's when I started thinking, "How are we going to get through this?" And that's what galvanized my thinking about the mayor's race.

MCDONALD: I read that you took your father-in-law to vote on election day.

LYLES: He is now ninety-four years old, and he has been one of my biggest supporters forever. He is as proud of me as my father would be. My father died at the age of sixty-five. But my father-in-law has been with me; he drove around, put up signs, and believed in me.

MCDONALD: So what does that mean to you, that someone who didn't have the right to vote for part of his life is now casting a ballot for you—for mayor?

LYLES: You always want to provide the people you love and respect with a reason to love and respect you. And that's what I felt with my father-in-law.

MCDONALD: You are the first African American woman mayor of Charlotte. Do you think that that distinction is important, significant? What's your reflection on that?

LYLES: I think it is significant. I meet young women, especially black and brown young women, and the first thing I say is, "I'm proud to be your mayor. And I'm doing this so that you can be governor or president."

I'm an instrument of our citizens, of the people who live here. You get elected, but that doesn't make you the conductor. What it makes you is first chair violin, and the conductor is the community. I listen really hard to what people are saying and doing in our city and what they want to happen. And my job is to figure out the best way to deliver the change that they want.

MCDONALD: One final question I have for you is, what keeps you grounded? What keeps you going?

LYLES: I am clear in my purpose and intent, but there are days that you get discouraged. If I have a long day, and I don't feel like it went well, I try to think, "Why? What happened? How did I lose my core?" And I try to think it through. I'm truly an optimist. I just know that if we give people the ability to have a safe place to live and a way to move around that we would be a better city. And I have a tangible love for my city. This is a place that I care deeply about, and that's what keeps me going.

This interview has been edited for length and clarity.
Carol McDonald is on the board of Higher Heights for America, which endorsed Mayor Lyles.

DIMPLE AJMERA

City Council // Charlotte, North Carolina // Elected in 2017

MY FAMILY IMMIGRATED TO THE United States from India when
I was sixteen. We were in search of better opportunities. We had just two
suitcases and no money. We didn't even speak the language.

My parents worked long and hard to provide for us. It wasn't always
easy. But still, they found the time and means to help others. They celebrated our birthdays by going out and feeding those who were homeless.
They worked at local charities. They promoted peace and nonviolence. And
they helped families after natural disasters.

In 2001, there was a huge earthquake in India. Tens of thousands of
people lost their lives. We were still living in the country at the time, and
my father was one of the leaders in the relief efforts. He helped rebuild a
city that had been destroyed.

We moved to the United States not long after that.

When I was in high school, my family had limited resources. I worked
part-time jobs to help make ends meet. At school, I received subsidized
lunches. I'd often bring part of my food home and share it with my family.
We were resilient. We survived as one team.

I also faced a steep language barrier. So, while all my classmates were
getting ready for prom, I was taking ESL classes. The first time I took my

English exam, I failed. I had never failed a test before. I started to doubt myself. But I worked hard and my teachers stayed after school to help me. The second time I took the exam, I passed.

I graduated from high school on time and I earned enough academic scholarships and financial aid to go to college. I had a brain for numbers and studied accounting at the University of Southern California (USC). Following in the footsteps of my parents, I found the time to work in the community. I taught classes at Title I schools. I worked as a volunteer at the National History Museum in Los Angeles and helped facilitate trips for underprivileged children. I even received the prestigious Volunteer Service Award from USC. My parents were so proud.

Those experiences opened my eyes to some of the inequities in this country. Not every family could afford to visit the museum. Not every school had the resources to help students, like me, learn English. For a lot of Americans, there are major barriers to opportunity.

After I graduated from college, I worked for big public accounting firms and became a CPA. Then I was recruited to Charlotte, North Carolina, to work for a Fortune 100 financial services firm. I had a good job making decent money.

I wanted to pay it forward, so I founded the Ajmera Scholarships. They provide financial assistance to underprivileged students at various educational institutions, as well as the Charlotte Housing Authority Scholarship Fund.

Life was good. I was giving a little back, working, making friends, and I was living the American dream. But then something happened. In 2013, my father, Tansen Ajmera, died suddenly of a heart attack. It shook me to my core.

I was tasked with writing his obituary. It was the first time I'd ever really thought seriously about death. I started thinking about my life and what I would leave behind when my time ended. I started thinking about how I wanted to spend my time now, so I could create a legacy to be proud of.

After my father passed, many of his friends called me. They talked about how much he'd done and how much he'd given. Meanwhile, I felt I had lost touch with what was really important. I had all of these opportunities and never really committed as much as I could for others. I'd lost touch with service. So, I asked myself: How could I carry on my father's legacy? How could I improve the lives of those around me? How could I build a brighter future for my community?

I would continue to fund the scholarships—now the Tansen Ajmera Scholarships, in honor of my father. But I really needed to do something more. After all, my father helped rebuild a city!

That's when I decided that it was time to be that same kind of leader. From then on, I would do everything I could to make Charlotte a place where everyone could succeed, no matter where they'd come from.

I got involved in a bunch of different things. I joined the Doing My Part Street Team to serve Charlotte's homeless community. I worked with the Aldersgate Retirement Community to serve senior citizens. I volunteered in the Charlotte-Mecklenburg schools to help educate our young people. I began attending the meetings of the Young Democrats of Mecklenburg County.

I just couldn't get enough—or do enough. Public service is in my blood.

Neighborhood leaders encouraged me to seek a board position with the Charlotte Housing Authority (CHA), which provides housing and supportive services to more than 25,000 individuals in Charlotte. This seemed perfect for me. I applied and was appointed by the city council and joined the board.

Serving on the CHA opened my eyes to the needs of people in my city. Of the fifty largest U.S. cities, Charlotte is ranked dead last in terms of upward mobility. So if you are living in poverty, you are likely to stay living in poverty. And housing is a primary factor. It impacts everything—where you go to school, what kind of transportation you use, where you shop, what you eat.

I really enjoyed that work. But still, I wanted to do more.

In 2016, my friend and mentor on the city council, John Autry, was elected to the North Carolina Statehouse. That created an open seat on the council. John lived in my district and community members asked me if I would be interested in filling his seat. At first I said no. But then, I shadowed John for almost a year.

I realized how important local government is in people's day-to-day lives. I thought I could add value and take on some important issues. So I

I JUST COULDN'T GET

ENOUGH

OR DO ENOUGH

PUBLIC

SERVICE

★ IS IN MY BLOOD ★

applied to fill his seat and, in January 2017, I was unanimously appointed by the city council. I became the first Asian American and the youngest woman ever to serve on the Charlotte city council.

Immediately, I began working on a project to create jobs, improve infrastructure, and help a neighborhood in East Charlotte. It's a part of our city that has been ignored for many years and also one of the most diverse. I knew that if we created more opportunities there, we could help stabilize the community and make it safer. We made tremendous strides in just a few months.

Still, I wanted to keep going. When one of my colleagues, Vi Lyles, decided to run for mayor, it created an open at-large seat on the city council. So I decided to run citywide.

There were eight Democrats, including three incumbents, running in the primary for four at-large seats. I got past that nail-biting hurdle. Then there were seven people total, Democrats and Republicans, running in the general election. Most of them had more resources than I did. All of them had been in Charlotte much longer than I had. But I worked hard, and I made it past that hurdle, too. I won!

When we moved to the United States, my parents had big dreams for us. I don't know if they could ever have dreamed of this. But I really owe it all to them; it's because of them that public service runs in my blood.

WILMOT COLLINS

Mayor // Helena, Montana // Elected in 2017

I GREW UP IN LIBERIA, WEST AFRICA.

I always wanted to get into politics. I studied political science and sociology and got my degree. A few years before I graduated, Master Sergeant Samuel Doe won an election and became president of Liberia. Under his regime, you either joined his political party or life as you knew it would be difficult.

So, after I graduated, I decided that I would attend the Liberian Foreign Service Institute. While I waited to get in, I started teaching at the SOS Children's Village in Monrovia.

Soon, however, my dreams of entering the foreign service faded. My country was being divided by a terrible civil war. Government officials were being killed, and so were rebel sympathizers.

My wife and I fled. We registered with the United Nations Refugee Agency and petitioned the United States government for refugee status, and, eventually, we landed in Helena, Montana.

This community gave me a chance, and I wanted to be a part of it. A full part of it. I got my first job. I got involved with the adult baseball league. I started coaching soccer. I became a member of the Covenant United Methodist Church and joined the choir. And I never looked back after that.

After a while, I started wondering how I could serve my community even more. I started thinking about entering politics. I even talked to my family about it, but every time the deadlines for running for office got close, I got cold feet. I knew the odds were stacked against me.

But 2017 was different. This time, my son wouldn't let me back out. He kept telling me that it was now or never. He kept reminding me that I could win.

We talked about it a bit more and, finally, I gathered my family and friends together. I wanted to get a feel for what they thought. A friend said, "It's time." They all agreed to help me and guide me through the process.

I remembered what President Barack Obama had said at the Democratic National Convention in 2016. He said, "Change can't happen without a lot of hard work from the ground up, from people like you and me."

That was it. I was running. For mayor of Helena, the community that provided me a chance. After I announced my candidacy, I was overwhelmed by support. I received encouraging letters from high school students and senior citizens. It seemed as if everyone wanted to help me by putting up flyers or stuffing envelopes or doing whatever they could. I had volunteers who were willing to walk in the rain to knock on doors. They knew that change would come from the ground up, and they wanted to make that change a reality.

Still, it was an uphill battle. I was running for office while the Trump administration was coming after refugees and immigrants. And I was running against an incumbent who was well liked.

There were times when it might have been easier to get out of the race, but I love my community. So many people were looking for new leadership, a new direction for our city; that kept me moving forward.

Running for office takes energy, commitment, and support. Lots of support. Financial and labor. Our municipal elections in Helena are nonpartisan. I had to find a way to meet with as many voters as possible. I teamed up with two others who were running for the city commission, and we set up meet-and-greets together. This was a good way to get to know people, but I was also aware that people—especially the media—were watching my every move.

I attended every public forum. I participated in everything I could—from events at local high schools to church group meetings. I knocked on as many doors as possible. That, I found, is the single best way to get your name out. You can't just leave a flyer. You've got to knock.

One time, I knocked on a door, and a nice couple answered. I saw my flyer on their dining room table. But, still, they didn't know I was running. We talked for about five minutes, and I learned that they were excited to have a choice in the upcoming election.

Another time when I knocked on another door, the woman who answered began grilling me. But then, her son, a high schooler, came to the door and said, "Hi, Mr. Collins. You spoke to my world cultures class last week." He turned to his mom and said, "He's cool, Mom. Vote for him." And that's what it took to win his mom over.

I left no stone unturned. I always reminded myself that I was the underdog, that I had an uphill battle, that nothing was enough.

Two days before the election, I told myself, "If I don't win, it's not because I didn't give it my all."

But more than twenty years after Helena gave me my first chance, they gave me a second one. I won.

KELSEY WAITS

School Board // Hastings, Minnesota // Elected in 2017

DEAR ABBY AND KIT,

When I was a little girl, I told my parents that I was going to be the first woman president. I was confident, brave, and willing to do whatever it took to achieve my dreams. Just like you. I know that may be difficult to believe about me, your stay-at-home mom, but it's true: I used to believe that I would conquer the world someday.

However, by the time I was a teenager, it had become clear to me that a woman who believed in herself was considered intimidating. It wasn't "normal" to be smarter, more driven, or more outspoken than the boys my age. No, these traits could result in being teased or bullied or called a bitch.

I wanted to avoid that. So I taught myself to hide those parts of me. I was afraid of standing out; I just wanted to blend in. I convinced myself that my voice wasn't needed and that other women were just better suited to take on leadership roles. But as much as I tried to hide it, that confident little girl who wanted to be president was always inside, looking for a reason to speak out.

You are that reason. After the 2016 presidential election, I was lost. I didn't know what to do. I was depressed and scared, but I tried to get through each day with a smile for you. I didn't want you to worry any more than you already were. I soon realized that I needed to do more than just vote. I needed to do whatever I could to make sure that your future would remain bright. That meant fighting for a safe and inclusive community for you to grow up in, a diverse and high-quality education for you to receive, and the rights that you should have over your own bodies. I needed to figure out how I could protect those things for you. I had never been politically active, so figuring out how to do that was overwhelming.

Cue the Women's March.

Marching with you will always be one of my favorite memories, and there is no one I would rather have marched with. As we stood in St. Paul with close to 100,000 marchers, I saw the power that we all have. I saw the things that we are capable of and the movement that was starting. The energy was amazing. All we had to do was stand together. It wasn't one person who held the power in that march; we all held a little of it, and it was up to all of us to carry it forward.

Watching you at the march empowered me more than you will ever know. There you were, just three and six years old, but you were fearless and strong. You were ready to take on the world. It was amazing not only to see you but to see myself in you. You reminded me that I had not always been afraid to speak up. I knew, in that moment, that it was time for me to find my voice again.

That day of the Women's March, a part of me woke up, a part that I did not realize was still there.

Just a few weeks later, I went to the airport to protest President Trump's ban on refugees from Muslim countries. It was a spontaneous action (completely unlike me) and an amazing experience. While we were there, a family of Middle Eastern descent came out of the airport. They looked at us and I saw relief in their faces. I watched the mother and father point us out to their child, and all three of them smiled. That image will stay with me for a lifetime. Our small action had made a difference to someone, and that was motivation to keep going.

I wanted to do more, but I didn't know what form that would take. People had suggested that I run for office, but that wasn't on my radar and felt impossible. I kept making excuses about why right now wasn't the right time for me. I told myself that I was too young, you were too young, I was too new to our city, and I wasn't qualified for an elected position.

As it turns out, only women worry about these things (especially the qualifications part). Women don't apply for jobs unless they meet all of the qualifications. We tend to hesitate because we see qualifications as rules. Men jump in because they see job qualifications as suggestions. Never hesitate. Be confident in yourself. You are amazing and capable of anything.

Part of the reason I felt unqualified to run for office was that I was overthinking it. When I thought of elected office, my mind immediately went to state legislative positions or higher. As I understood it, those were the positions that made the most impact on our community. But then I discovered Run For Something. The group helped me understand the impact that local elected officials can have, and their goal is to prepare a progressive bench of eager young leaders at that level. That made sense and inspired me. I wanted to be a part of that bench.

So I decided to run for school board. Almost.

The hardest part about running for office was overcoming my own fears about not being qualified. Our filing period was two weeks long. I checked every day to see how many candidates had filed to run; I was watching the list closely. Every day of those two weeks I told myself that I wasn't qualified to be a school board member. Every day I hesitated, except the last one.

On that day, without thinking twice, I went to our district office and filed my paperwork. It was the best decision that I could have made. I didn't give myself time to second-guess the decision or to make excuses. It was done. And it turns out, that was all I needed. After filing, I was committed and immediately gave everything to running a strong campaign. In fact, I applied for three separate endorsements that very night.

When I told people that I was running for office, I was surprised at the amount of support I got. I received endorsements, financial support, and mentorship from multiple groups. Friends I hadn't seen in a decade rallied to support me in any way that they could. People believed in me and I started to believe in myself. I let my strong, confident personality come out. To my surprise, not only was I accepted, I was elected.

I have always tried to encourage you to ask questions and to be confident in yourselves. You are strong and smart and capable of anything, and there is nothing wrong with those qualities.

I used to think that your generation would change the social stigma surrounding strong women and that we just needed to wait for your generation to grow up. I used to think that the world would be ready for you in a way that it wasn't ready for me. What I didn't realize is that the world is ready now. We don't need to wait—you or me. The world needs brave women who will step out of their comfort zones and take leadership roles at their schools, in their jobs, in their communities, and in their government. We need to not only hear more voices of women, we need to listen to them.

Instead of telling ourselves that we aren't qualified, women need to look at our perceived weaknesses in a new light. In our house, when you say something negative about yourself, you know that you have to turn around and tell me three things that you like about yourself instead. I want you to focus on your strengths. When I ran for office, that's exactly what I did.

My "weaknesses" not only turned into strengths, they became the platform for my entire campaign and the very reasons that people voted for me.

Originally, I said that I was "too young" and "too new to our community." I am young and I am new to our community, but should those facts be considered weaknesses? I am a young mother. That means that I have a vested interest in this school system and this community that someone from an older generation might not. After researching the area, it also turns out that the twenty-to-thirty-year-old demographic in our community is shrinking. We are failing to attract new, young families to this city. But here I was, a new, young woman who'd chosen to move here with her family. I chose this city for a reason, and if I did, then others could, as well. I have a voice and a unique perspective that our local government needs right now.

Another unique perspective when running for school board was the fact that we homeschool. We never planned on homeschooling, but it was the right decision for you and for our family. Our experience makes me a stronger advocate for supportive student environments, especially as mental health problems in children continue to rise. Again, I turned a perceived weakness into a strength and looked past what I believed were the "necessary qualifications" to hold elected office.

I could not have done any of this without you. You were my rocks. You constantly inspire me and motivate me to keep going. Every time that I thought I was too tired to door-knock, I just had to remember you. Thinking of your future kept me focused.

You were the best campaign helpers that I could have asked for; you were (almost) always excited to help and you even door-knocked with me (almost) every day. You made campaigning more fun than I could have imagined. We made some wonderful memories that months later we are still laughing about. As an introvert, I never would have guessed that I would have enjoyed campaigning as much as I did. I also wouldn't have guessed that just two weeks later, you would be asking me when we could start door-knocking again. You are amazing.

A few months after the election, you and I were having a discussion in the car about superheroes. I told you that I liked Batman because he was just a regular person (albeit a billionaire), but he still wanted to change the world for the better. You told me that he was like me because I was also a regular person and a superhero. I almost cried. Being your hero is the greatest honor of my life. I will do everything that I can to keep you safe and to make you proud. I love you more than you will ever know. Thank you for believing in me.

Love,
Mom

ANNA V. ESKAMANI

House of Representatives // Florida's 47th House District //
Elected in 2018

THERE WAS NOT JUST ONE moment in my life or one person who inspired me to lead. I am the sum of those around me, and there are many who deserve mention as motivators and mentors in my growth as a leader and now candidate. From them, I have learned that leadership rises in moments of uncertainty.

My life has been full of uncertain moments.

I was born and raised in Orlando by a working-class family of immigrants. I have a twin sister and an older brother. My mom is a force of nature and was the first person who encouraged me to lead.

She grew up in Iran and immigrated to the United States as a young woman decades ago. Despite having acquired a college degree in Iran, she was never able to secure a job here that accepted her international credentials. Instead, she worked minimum-wage jobs at fast-food restaurants and eventually was a department manager at a local Kmart.

That would be her last job, because in 2004, after a five-year battle with cancer, my mom died. I was thirteen years old.

Not only was I thirteen years old without a mom, but I was thirteen years old, without a mom, and about to enter high school. My period had not even started yet, and I had never dated or even kissed a boy. I was trying to fit in and did not know if I would.

I found power in my pain and made it my responsibility to make sure that no one else felt the way that I did. Which is probably why when I met my first openly gay friend, Aaron, we clicked instantly. He was figuring stuff out, too, managing his own lived experiences. We both also thought the same boy was cute, so we had a lot in common.

Aaron introduced me to high school theater.

Theater and the arts became a space for me to grow as a young leader and develop skills that I never thought I had—from building set pieces to creating props and costumes to leading shows backstage alongside other techies. I learned how to trust my intuition, work in teams, and manage crises.

Theater was my main focus while in high school, and though I maintained strong progressive values, I was not really politically engaged.

That was until I met Mr. Norris, my AP American government teacher. He was a white, middle-aged man who spoke truth to power in his classroom. He shared stories of marginalized communities, spoke to societal injustices, and painted a picture of potential for my generation. Mr. Norris, coupled with the movement behind President Obama's first presidential election, got me into the fold, and I knew going into college I wanted to engage with civics.

I stayed local and went to the University of Central Florida (UCF) for college. My dad had gone to UCF, as had my brother, so it was a natural fit for my twin sister and me. UCF is the largest university in Florida and the second largest in the country. It is a big campus, with big ideas.

On this campus, I evolved from an arts-loving theater kid to an effective and bold organizer who challenged the status quo and encouraged her classmates to do the same. The lessons that Mr. Norris taught me came to life as I witnessed inequities in my own life and the lives of others.

While an undergrad at UCF, I first focused my energy on environmental issues, then on international human rights, and finally on advocating for domestic issues and women's rights via the College Democrats at UCF and the Florida College Democrats.

We organized town halls, rallies, voter registration drives, and forums to help students understand their own efficacy. My theater skills came in handy, as we would host large-scale events with logistics, supplies, and risks not unlike those of hosting a performance. The main difference: This show was real life, and the stakes were high.

I graduated from UCF with two bachelor's degrees, one in political science and the other in women's studies. I returned to complete two master's and am now a PhD student. UCF not only gave me the opportunity to grow as a leader; it's also where I first heard the phrase "the personal is political"—a rallying cry that impacts me to this day.

When I was an undergraduate, I learned about Planned Parenthood. In case you don't know, Planned Parenthood is a leading provider of reproductive health care, education, and advocacy. While I got a great education in theater and government, there was no sexual health education at my high school. As a young woman dating for the first time, without knowledge of consent or contraception, that put me at a big disadvantage.

Searching for answers, I went to Planned Parenthood.

They provided me with the information I needed to be healthy and strong and have access to a method of birth control that was right for me. I was inspired by the work of Planned Parenthood, so inspired that I started making small donations and volunteered as a health center escort, walking patients in when there were protesters outside.

In 2012, I was offered a job at my local Planned Parenthood affiliate. I accepted that job, and six years later, I now serve as a senior director overseeing public policy and communications work across twenty-two counties and eleven health centers.

My work at Planned Parenthood in a state like Florida opened my eyes to both the hostile political climate we're in and the stigma that patients must navigate just to access what should be basic health care.

I witnessed firsthand the legislature's distaste toward women and its efforts to dismantle our rights. I met with legislators, empowered patients to share their stories, and watched year after year as laws were passed that continued to treat women, people of color, members of the LGBTQ community, and those with disabilities as if we were all second-class citizens.

It gave me a front-row seat to the uncertainty that many Floridians face. That uncertainty got worse with the election of President Donald Trump.

His election should not have surprised me.

I remember chuckling when a Republican friend told me he was supporting Donald Trump. He referred to him as a "long shot" but still felt he was the best man for the job. The closer that came to becoming a reality, the more urgency I felt to stop it. I organized against Trump on the ground in Central Florida, and after he won, I kept on going.

At Planned Parenthood, the calls and emails from patients, donors, and volunteers would not stop. To meet this fierce demand, we organized nine volunteer orientations in eight cities across twenty-two counties in just three weeks. Then came the Women's March and the Muslim ban. We organized, organized, organized.

In the middle of all that, it dawned on me that nothing would change unless we elected the right people. Nothing would change unless we built a bench of strong progressive candidates in Florida who would not only run for office but also teach and train others to do the same.

I knew that it needed to start with me.

I launched my campaign on July 3, 2017. In just a few months, we raised hundreds of thousands of dollars, knocked on thousands of doors, qualified for the ballot by petition, and won the endorsements of more than forty community leaders and organizations. I was also one of the forty-eight women featured on the January 2018 cover of *Time* magazine.

Running for office takes being yourself. It takes remembering where you come from and who you are. It takes grit and grace. It takes asking for guidance but also trusting your gut.

I am grateful for the experiences that have built me and for the people who have invested their time, energy, and love to turn me into a leader. Leadership rises in moments of uncertainty, but you never have to rise up alone. Bring others with you, and don't leave anyone behind.

NOTHING
WOULD CHANGE
★ UNLESS WE ★
ELECTED
 THE ◄►
RIGHT PEOPLE

MAI KHANH TRAN
with Jack Hipkins

U.S. House of Representatives //
California's 39th Congressional District // Candidate in 2018

WHEN I WAS IN JUNIOR HIGH SCHOOL, I decided to run for student body president. I had to give a speech. I don't remember much of it, but I do remember the quote I used. It was from Bobby Kennedy:

There are those who look at things the way they are and ask, "Why?"
I dream of things that never were and ask, "Why not?"

I remember how I felt walking out onto the stage—my hands sweaty, my stomach tying itself into knots. Standing in front of five hundred schoolmates, about to give the first speech of my life, I could feel my heart rattling my chest with each beat and my head pounding along in time.

I was scared. I was a refugee from Vietnam who had only been in the United States for three years. Who was I to run? Who was I to think that I had a chance to win?

But I looked around my school and saw the way things were. And then I looked around my school and dreamed of how things could be. There were things that could be done to make our school better than it was, but no one was willing to step up and get them done.

I decided I had to run, to be a voice calling for the change that I knew our school needed. Honestly, I didn't think I could win, but I hoped that at the very least I could show my classmates the vision I had for the future of our school and maybe, just maybe, see some of that vision become reality.

So, despite the fear, I walked out onto that stage, and I put my heart and soul into that speech. And I achieved the unexpected.

I won.

I came to the United States as part of the orphan airlift after the fall of Saigon in 1975. When I first arrived with my siblings, we didn't know if we would ever see our parents again. My father had dropped us off at an orphanage several weeks before, knowing that in the event of an evacuation the Americans would make sure that orphans got out of the country. He was willing to risk permanent separation from his children in order to give us a chance at a better life. Thankfully, my parents were able to escape Vietnam, and we were reunited in Portland, Oregon, one year later.

Not even a week after we arrived in Portland, I was enrolled at one of the local elementary schools. I joined school in the middle of fifth grade and was immediately dropped into a full course load taught entirely in English.

I didn't speak a single word of English.

Those first weeks were among some of the most difficult of my life. I was unable to talk to anyone or understand what was happening. But my parents taught us the importance of education. So, each and every day, I spent each and every minute of spare time studying and learning English. By the end of the year, I was one of the top students in my class.

In sixth grade I transferred to Glenhaven Junior High. The school was incredibly diverse. The student body was made up of mostly native-born Americans, but about a quarter of the students were refugees like me from Vietnam and other Southeast Asian countries. We also had a significant number of African American students bused in from other communities.

In those first two years at Glenhaven, I began to identify the issues that faced our school. With a large number of refugee students entering the school at all times of the year, I realized we needed services to help new immigrants learn English and integrate into the school environment. There were numerous problems within student government, from disorganized weekly meetings to underfunded school events. But most of all,

I felt that, as students, we didn't have a unified voice to communicate our concerns to school administrators.

Toward the beginning of eighth grade, when the time rolled around for student elections, I had no intention of running for student body president. But when I saw the candidates who were declaring, I realized they all represented more of the same. They were running to be popular, to bolster their profile for future college applications, or even just for the fun of it. We didn't need more of the same. We needed change. So I put aside my reservations and threw my name into the ring.

That experience running in junior high school had a profound impact on me. It taught me that if you wanted to change something in your community, you had to have the guts to stand up and be the person to lead the change. And it also gave me hope for the future. I believed that we could change the world.

After I graduated from high school, I decided to pursue pediatrics as my way to create positive change in the world. I had a great job, a rewarding one. I had everything I needed.

Until November 9, 2016.

I was so distraught that all I wanted to do was curl up in my bed and pretend that things had gone differently the night before. But I had to go to work, and I knew my patients needed me that day like any other. So I did what many women did all across the country—I got up, got dressed, and went out to take care of my family and my patients.

Walking into my office that day, it felt as if everyone was in mourning. My staff was in tears, and everyone greeted one another with a hug.

The first patient I saw was a five-year-old girl whose face was disfigured because of an advanced brain tumor. Her family had obtained health insurance only two months earlier, as a result of the subsidies provided by the Affordable Care Act.

I spent the morning crying with the girl and her mother. With the Republicans in control of the White House and both houses of Congress, we knew their family could lose the health-care coverage they'd just gotten.

I knew I had to do something. I knew I had to do more than simply be a pediatrician. I needed to fight to protect women and children across California and throughout America.

WE DREAMED
OF A
BETTER
FUTURE

I saw our country for what it was, and I dreamed of a country where my patient and her mother, and people all across this nation, would never again have to worry about having access to affordable health care. And I realized that if I wanted to make that dream into a reality, I would have to step up and run for Congress.

In 2017, I spoke at the California Democratic Party convention, at the Asian American and Pacific Islander Caucus. In my speech, I focused on inspiration. I told them that in order for Democrats to take back the House in 2018, we would have to inspire the American people. We would have to inspire people who don't normally vote to get up, go out, and vote. We would have to inspire people to vote for higher ideals—ideals that extend far beyond one election.

I told them that if we worked hard, we could beat the odds. Why? Because we dreamed of a better future. A future without prejudice or injustice. A future when we take care of one another. A future when we place the good of all before the greed of a few. A future when everyone is welcome, when everyone can succeed. That's our dream.

As Bobby Kennedy said, "There are those who look at things the way they are and ask, 'Why?'"

We dream of things that never were, and ask, "Why not?"

TYLER TITUS

School Board // Erie, Pennsylvania // Elected in 2017

MY CAMPAIGN MANAGER, ALAYNA, leaned over and grabbed my hand. She looked up from her phone—she had been tracking the polls as the results rolled in—and said, "It's time to call it." I stood up and walked to the front of the room. The room full of my close friends and family fell silent as they watched me climb on top of a chair.

I had thought about this moment for months. But when I looked out at the faces of those who had rallied around me through this whole campaign for school board, my mind went blank, my heart began racing, and my eyes welled up. I cleared my throat and let the words fall out.

"The numbers keep coming in and the divide between the candidates continues to grow. It's clear now that catching up isn't feasible." I paused and smiled. "We did it. We made history."

Everything after that moment melds together in an emotional blur. I know I kept talking, but I don't know what else I said. I remember the sound of cheering. The hugs and handshakes seemed to follow one right after the other. I remember that I couldn't stop smiling and that there were surges of surrealism. Within the hour, I was receiving waves of social media posts and texts and voicemail messages.

These messages varied from congratulating me to warning me to degrading me. As a transgender male, I knew that the responses to my election would be charged with positive and negative reactions. So I braced myself for the anger and hatred.

This wasn't the first time in my life I had been the recipient of hostility and rejection. In fact, I had spent much of my adolescence subjected to bullying simply for being perceived as different. I wasn't "out" as trans or queer during high school, but that didn't prevent the rumors from spreading or stop my peers from chasing me into bathrooms while taunting me. "Just wait until I find you alone," they'd say.

Despite all of that, here I was, making history. I knew this election held great significance for numerous reasons: I was the first openly transgender candidate elected to public office in the state of Pennsylvania. And I was one of many transgender candidates who won in states across the country on November 7, 2017. The nation was watching and the energy was building. People wanted to hear from me.

During the first thirty-six hours after the results circulated, I knew that my election was part of a movement. I needed to decide what I wanted my role to be. I was standing at the forefront of change and I was given a voice.

At times, I experienced significant self-doubt. I questioned my ability to be a voice and a face for my community. And in my darkest moments, I even considered retreating back into silence.

But then I remembered the loneliness I'd felt as a child knowing I wasn't like the other kids. If I close my eyes, I can still feel the ache of wanting to be accepted, believing if those around me would just open their hearts, they would see that my differences made me beautiful. I would dream of finding people who could see me for who I was and not fixate on who they wanted me to be.

I thought of the children who still sit alone in their bedrooms today, daydreaming the same way I did, hoping that someday someone would do something. I remembered that I am somebody and I can do something. I can be an agent of change, and I can work to transform how others are seen and treated. I can keep pushing the barriers created by ignorance and fear, because there are people who do not have the privilege to push against the systems that hold them down.

Before I ran, before I won, two of my friends made the decision to end their own lives. They were both in their twenties, full of promise. But because they were transgender women, they were held in an oppressed state that simply became too much to bear. Their letters outlined how exhausted they had become from fighting to be accepted and understood. Their experience cannot continue to be the story that our youth hears or takes on as their own truth. We cannot let our children believe that we exist in a time that is so hateful that the only resolution is ending their own lives.

Changing the trajectory for our children is why I chose to run for office, and for school board in particular. I am aware of the privilege I experience from my support system, and I will not ever let it be lost on me. I have amazing people in my life who continue to love me unconditionally. It is with their help that I can stand up and push forward.

I have been told that I am brave. I do not feel brave. I do feel compelled to change the perception of what it means to be a leader who is also transgender. So often those who identify or express themselves in a way that deviates from the social norm are asked to take labels that are just as limiting as the ones they just shed. We are taken from one box and shoved into another.

When I was young, my father and stepmother were appalled by the tomboy, country, spirited child they would pick up for their court-ordered visits. I would have to change out of my clothes and into ones that they believed were appropriate. They boxed me into what they believed a daughter should be. My classmates felt similarly. I didn't act like "the other girls," and they used words, fists, and isolation to try to shove me back into their comfort zone.

When I came out as a lesbian, I was told how lesbians should act and be. When I came out as transgender, I was assigned male pronouns and quickly began to realize that I did not match society's expectations of men. I was too effeminate.

When I became a parent, I was first seen as a mother. My gentleness was expected. No one complimented me for hugging my children. Now that I am seen as the father I am, I often get positive feedback on what a loving, kind, affectionate father I am to my boys. Societal norms, and misguided gender judgments, are placed upon even our most intimate relationships.

So, you see, I have lived much of my life in—and climbing out of—boxes I never asked to be placed in.

During my campaign, I was the Trans-Candidate. I spent a great deal of time shifting the discussion back to the reasons why I was running and not allowing people to push me into the "trans-candidate" box.

To win an election in which you are challenging comfort levels and social inequities, you need to do more than push limits. You need to shatter them. You need to know who you are and what you value. Then, when the inevitable ignorance comes, you have to persevere and resist being defined only by your body or your gender.

The 2017 elections were undeniably important for those facing discrimination and inequality. I know it is essential for me to be open about my transition, taking this opportunity to change minds. I also know it is of equal importance to let others see who I am and what I stand for. I will not be shoved back into a single definition.

I am somebody who possesses many traits and skills. I am a transgender male. I am a father of two beautiful little boys. I am the oldest brother to thirteen siblings. I am an uncle to seven nieces and nephews. I am a therapist to those who have been hurt by the world around them. I am an advocate and a voice for the quieted. I am an elected official. I am a school board member. I am all these things and more. I am Tyler Titus.

I am you. For despite all our differences, we are one united force. And together, we will take down the political powers that oppress us. We will keep making history.

WE DID IT

WE MADE

HISTORY

Resources

THINKING ABOUT RUNNING FOR OFFICE? Here are a few
organizations that can help.

AAPI Victory Fund // aapivictoryfund.com
*"The AAPI Victory Fund . . . is focused on mobilizing Asian American and
Pacific Islanders (AAPI) eligible voters and moving them to the ballot box."*

The Collective PAC // collectivepac.org
*"Our mission is to build Black political power, and through our various
entities, we do this through educating and equipping voters, donors, and
candidates with various resources including trainings, technical assistance, paid communications, and fundraising."*

Emerge America // emergeamerica.org
*"Emerge America is changing the face of politics by recruiting, training,
and providing a powerful network for Democratic women to run
for office."*

EMILY's List // emilyslist.org
*"We ignite change by getting pro-choice Democratic women elected
to office."*

Higher Heights for America // higherheightsforamerica.org
*"Higher Heights is the only national organization providing Black women
with a political home exclusively dedicated to harnessing their power to
elect Black women, influence elections, and advance progressive policies."*

Latino Victory Project // latinovictory.us
*"Latino Victory is a progressive organization working to grow Latino
political power by increasing Latino representation at every level
of government and building a base of Latino donors to support this
critical work."*

National Democratic Training Committee // traindemocrats.org
"We offer any Democratic candidate running for office, up and down the ticket, free online campaign training."

Rise to Run // risetorun.org
"Rise to Run brings progressive girls and young women together in their communities to give them insight into the political process, connect them with mentors, and involve them in local organizing."

Run for Something // runforsomething.net
"Run for Something recruits and supports young, diverse, progressive individuals to run for state and local offices to build a bench for the future—the folks we support now could be possible members of the House, Senate, and maybe even President one day."

She Should Run // sheshouldrun.org
"Our mission is to expand the talent pool of women running for office in the United States by providing community, resources, and growth opportunities for aspiring political leaders."

Victory Fund // victoryfund.org
"LGBTQ Victory Fund works to change the face and voice of America's politics and achieve equality for LGBTQ Americans by increasing the number of openly LGBTQ officials at all levels of government."

VoteRunLead // voterunlead.org
"VoteRunLead trains women to run for office. And win."

"NEVER STOP
BELIEVING
THAT FIGHTING FOR
WHAT'S RIGHT
 IS
WORTH IT"
—HILLARY CLINTON

Acknowledgments

SO MANY PEOPLE MADE THIS BOOK POSSIBLE—my editor, Samantha Weiner; my agent, Jessica Regel; my collaborators at In This Together Media, Carey Albertine and Saira Rao; and the whole crew at Abrams Books. Thank you.

I am grateful to U.S. Senator Tammy Duckworth and all of the contributors—Stacey Abrams, Amy McGrath, Kwame Raoul, Helen Gym, Ashley Bennett, Zach Wahls, Saira Rao, Barbara Lee, Daniel Hernández Jr., Heather Ward, Sheila Oliver, Debra Haaland, Valerie Hefner, Michelle Lujan Grisham and Stephanie Schriock, Jason Kander, Jennifer Carroll Foy, Pramila Jayapal, Alexandra Chandler, Shoshanna Kelly, Kate Brown, Michelle De La Isla, Andrew Gillum, Nelson Araujo, Jenny Durkan, Andrea Jenkins, Karen Caudillo, Tom Perriello, Kevindaryán Luján, Vi Lyles and Carol McDonald, Dimple Ajmera, Wilmot Collins, Kelsey Waits, Anna V. Eskamani, Mai Khanh Tran and Jack Hipkins, and Tyler Titus. Thank you for running in the first place and for sharing your stories here.

As a former staffer myself, I also have to give a shout-out to the staffers of the contributors, who work so hard to help elect progressive candidates to public office (and who, less importantly, fielded countless e-mails, calls, and texts from me).

Ross Morales Rocketto of Run for Something, Christina Reynolds of EMILY's List, Carol McDonald of Higher Heights for America, and so many other leaders in the progressive movement helped me along the way. I also couldn't have done this without the support of my team at West Wing Writers.

With love, I have to thank my village, my godmother, Mary, my partner, Ariana, and our son, Asher.

In solidarity, I have to thank everyone who is keeping up the fight and Hillary Clinton, who told us, "Never stop believing that fighting for what's right is worth it."

It is worth it.

About the Editor

KATE CHILDS GRAHAM is a political speechwriter. She served as communications director for U.S. Senator Amy Klobuchar. She also wrote speeches for principals and surrogates during the Clinton-Kaine campaign and the 2016 Democratic National Convention. Currently, she is a principal at West Wing Writers.

Kate began her career writing and working in the labor, progressive faith, and reproductive health movements. For many years she wrote a regular column for the *National Catholic Reporter*, and she has appeared on MSNBC and CNN. She lives in Mount Rainier, Maryland, with her partner, Ariana, and their son.

About In This Together Media

IN THIS TOGETHER MEDIA develops books with greater diversity for the children's and adult markets. *Fast Company* has called In This Together Media one of their "Most Creative People." In This Together Media was selected as one of the five ventures for the SheEO award. The cofounders are Carey Albertine and Saira Rao.

Editor: Samantha Weiner
Designer: Danielle Youngsmith
Production Manager: Mike Kaserkie

Library of Congress Control Number: 2018953958

ISBN: 978-1-4197-3496-0
eISBN: 978-1-68335-499-4

Photo Credits
© Ben Garmisa, 6; © Stacey Abrams, 16; © Amy McGrath for Congress, 22; © Raoul for Illinois campaign, 28; © Kelly A. Burkhardt, 34; © courtesy of Ashley Bennett, 42; © Committee to Elect Zach Wahls, 48; © Ali Bibbo, 54; courtesy of Barbara Lee, 58; courtesy of Daniel Hernandez Jr., 65; courtesy of Heather Ward, 71; © Murphy for Governor, 76; © Deb Haaland for Congress, 82; © Angel Rowell Troxell, 88; © Michelle Lujan·Grisham, 94; © Jerry Schmidt, 104; © Mike C. Beaty, 110; © Pramila for Congress, 116; © Timothy Estey, 124; © Gregory Indruk, 132; © Izzy Ventura Meda, 138; © Ryan Bishop, 144; © Matt Burke, 150; © Committee to Elect Nelson Araujo, 156; © Joe Veyera, 162; © Brooke Ross, 168; courtesy of Karen Caudillo, 175; © Tom Perriello, 180; courtesy of Kevindaryán Luján, 188; © Vi Lyles for Mayor of Charlotte Campaign, 194; courtesy of Dimple Ajmera, 200; courtesy of Wilmot Collins, 206; courtesy of Kelsey Waits, 210; courtesy of Anna V. Eskamani, 216; © Dr. Mai Khanh Tran for Congress, 222; © Photography by Niko, 228.

Cover © 2019 Abrams

Printed and bound in USA
10 9 8 7 6 5 4 3 2 1

Abrams Image books are available at special discounts when purchased in quantity for premiums and promotions as well as fundraising or educational use. Special editions can also be created to specification. For details, contact specialsales@abramsbooks.com or the address below.

Abrams Image® is a registered trademark of Harry N. Abrams, Inc.

ABRAMS The Art of Books
195 Broadway, New York, NY 10007
abramsbooks.com